TAKING OFF THE
LIMITATIONS

DESTINY IMAGE BOOKS BY KEVIN L. ZADAI

TAKING OFF THE
LIMITATIONS

YOU CAN'T EVEN IMAGINE WHAT
GOD HAS IN STORE FOR YOU

KEVIN L. ZADAI

DESTINY IMAGE® PUBLISHERS, INC.

P.O. Box 310, Shippensburg, PA 17257-0310

"Promoting Inspired Lives."

This book and all other Destiny Image and Destiny Image Fiction books are available at Christian bookstores and distributors worldwide.

Cover design by Eileen Rockwell

For more information on foreign distributors, call 717-532-3040.

Reach us on the Internet: www.destinyimage.com.

ISBN 13 TP: 978-0-7684-5956-2
ISBN 13 eBook: 978-0-7684-5957-9
ISBN 13 HC: 978-0-7684-5959-3
ISBN 13 LP: 978-0-7684-5958-6

For Worldwide Distribution, Printed in the U.S.A.

1 2 3 4 5 6 7 8 / 25 24 23 22 21

DEDICATION

I dedicate this book to the Lord Jesus Christ. When I died during surgery and met with Jesus on the other side, He insisted that I return to life on the earth and that I help people with their destinies. Because of Jesus' love and concern for people, the Lord has actually chosen to send a person back from death to help everyone who will receive that help so that his or her destiny and purpose is secure in Him. I want You, Lord, to know that when You come to take me to be with You someday, it is my sincere hope that people remember not me, but the revelation of Jesus Christ that You have revealed through me. I want others to know that I am merely being obedient to Your heavenly calling and mission, which is to reveal Your plan for the fulfillment of the divine destiny for each of God's children.

ACKNOWLEDGMENTS

In addition to sharing my story with everyone through my previous books, the Lord gave me the commission to produce this book, *Taking Off the Limitations: You Can't Even Imagine What God Has for You*. This book addresses some of the revelations concerning the areas that Jesus reviewed and revealed to me through the Word of God and by the Spirit of God during several visitations. I want to thank everyone who has encouraged me, assisted me, and prayed for me during the writing of this work, especially my spiritual parents, Dr. Jesse Duplantis and Dr. Cathy Duplantis. Special thanks to my wonderful wife, Kathi, for her love and dedication to the Lord and me. Thank you, Sid Roth and staff, for your love of our supernatural Messiah, Jesus. Thank you, Warrior Notes staff, for the wonderful job editing this book. Thank you, Destiny Image and staff, for your support of this project. Special thanks as well, to all my friends who know about how to *Take Off the Limitations* and live the way Jesus would have us to live in the next move of God's Spirit!

CONTENTS

FOREWORD

H
OW HONORED I was when asked by my good friend Dr. Kevin Zadai to write a foreword for his new book. Dr. Kevin is a man on a mission from Heaven. After his encounter with Jesus, he began to move in his calling and is constantly moving up into higher levels of glory and gifting. He is here for such a time as this. He is an apostolic leader and a prophetic voice to the nations. Kevin and his wife, Kathi, have pioneered a ministry school that is at this time growing in numbers and enrollment beyond anything that I have ever seen. Dr. Kevin has been writing books about Jesus and the revelation that he receives for years. His writings are timeless treasures with eye-opening revelations.

Every book, every teaching, every conference, and every time he speaks has a touch of God's heavenly glory on it. Dr. Kevin Zadai and Kathi are world-class leaders sent to train and equip a whole generation for the next new move of God. Kevin carries a mantle from Heaven itself and he teaches and writes in that heavenly atmosphere. This book, like all others he has authored, is another timeless treasure filled with divine truths and revelations. When I think about how God is using Dr. Kevin and Kathi, the word that comes to me is *incalculable*. It means the scope and destiny of their work is incalculable—it's endless, immeasurable, limitless, and uncountable.

When I think that they have a destiny to fulfill, it literally causes me to praise God for what's about to happen in their life and ministry. I am immediately drawn to Genesis 22, to the story of Abraham and Sarah. Abraham had just passed the greatest test of his life. The Bible teaches us that the Lord wanted to give him a reward. And in Genesis 22:15-17, the angel of the Lord came to Abraham out of Heaven and called a second time and said, *"Blessing I will bless you, and multiplying I will multiply your descendants as the stars of the heaven and as the sand which is on the seashore."* In other words, your calling will leave a destiny and impact on the earth that is incalculable—limitless, endless, and timeless. That is what is happening with Dr. Kevin and Kathi Zadai—they are on a mission for Jesus to bless a whole generation to do what Jesus did.

This book will bring the world into the vision that Jesus carried and that Kevin carries. I just want to thank the Lord for this opportunity to write about this book. This is not just a book but an encounter with the deeper things of the Lord Jesus Christ.

DR. KEITH ELLIS, TH.D.
Prophet

INTRODUCTION

THE LORD JESUS spent precious time with His disciples, mentoring them to take over His ministry before leaving the earth to return to the Father. We now have the same Great Commission to do the works of Jesus and even greater works because He returned to Heaven. Remember, Jesus never limited anyone when it came to their faith. In Mark 9:23, He said that nothing was impossible to him who believes. In 1992 during my heavenly visitation, I saw that no one in Heaven was limiting me, including the angels sent to help me and the Holy Spirit inside of me. The cloud of witnesses is cheering us on right now, and the saints know that the limitations have been taken off! Let the Spirit of God set you free as you read this timely message.

God bless!

DR. KEVIN ZADAI, TH.D.

Chapter 1

WHY IS MY WORLD SO SMALL?

GETTING RID OF ME, MYSELF, AND I

And raised us up together, and made us sit together in the heavenly places in Christ Jesus, that in the ages to come He might show the exceeding riches of His grace in His kindness toward us in Christ Jesus.
—EPHESIANS 2:6-7

THERE IS A council that meets in Heaven that decides the things of the kingdom of God before they ever happen. That truth that has been established in Heaven then needs to be implemented in this realm. On this earth, we need people who know how to walk with God and implement God's will as ambassadors for Heaven. There are many different ways that this can be done. We can do it through prayer, we can do it through speaking, and we can do it through actions. There are so many different ways to implement the kingdom and God's desires into this realm. The greatest thing about God is that He has a big heart, and He has an intention for humanity that goes beyond description.

I have never been able to express what I saw in Heaven fully. The Word of God is there in front of you, but there is so much more that you have to understand and speak and pray out. Heaven is so big, and God's heart is so big. God loves you so much, but a lot of times His intentions toward you are not known, and therefore they cannot be implemented. Not many believers have fully realized what God has for them. What God has for you is so much more than you could ever think or ask. If you, as one person, could grasp the fullness of what God has for you, it would change history, and everyone would know who you were.

> *And He said to me, "My grace is sufficient for you, for My strength is made perfect in weakness." Therefore most gladly I will rather boast in my infirmities, that the power of Christ may rest upon me. Therefore I take pleasure in infirmities, in reproaches, in needs, in persecutions, in distresses, for Christ's sake. For when I am weak, then I am strong.*
> —2 CORINTHIANS 12:9-10

The Lord Jesus has asked me not to focus on people's weaknesses but to focus on their strengths. You must let God come into your weaknesses and strengthen you so that you can be an overcomer in this life. When you receive overcoming power and you overcome, you are also going *to be* overcome. Understand that God's perception of things is a lot higher than ours, and His ways are higher. The key down here is not to see God working but to be part of it. We are not supposed to be spectators, but we are supposed to be participators. We are supposed to know His ways, which means that we are implementers.

Jesus Himself told me that the limitations had been taken off my life. Now there are obvious limitations of life here on earth, such as living in an earthly body that will one day die. If you are born again, your spirit has been redeemed by the blood of Jesus. Your soul, which is your mind, will, and emotions, is being transformed and renewed daily by the power of the Word of God, which frames our mindset. Other than these, Jesus told me that the limitations have been taken off.

When Jesus was raised up, He raised us up with Him. I saw all of this when I was in Heaven, and I saw that it takes participation. This raising up is God's intention for us, and it is part of His ways. It is not something that we are just spectators of, for we must participate in the raising up of ourselves into the heavenly realms. You must see God working in your life every day, and you should be aware of God's angels working in your life to help you to implement those things.

The Pharisees were part of a system that God instituted in the desert with Moses. However, the Pharisees became a religious system that was not faithful to help God's people. They put yokes on the people instead of taking them off and brought the people into bondage. The law was in place to curb sin and discourage people from doing the wrong thing and encourage them to do the right thing.

> *Now it shall come to pass, if you diligently obey the voice of the Lord your God, to observe carefully all His commandments which I command you today, that the Lord your God will set you high above all nations of the earth. And all these blessings shall come upon you and overtake you, because you obey the voice of the Lord your God.*
> —DEUTERONOMY 28:1-2

> *But it shall come to pass, if you do not obey the voice of the Lord your God, to observe carefully all His commandments and His statutes which I command you today, that all these curses will come upon you and overtake you.*
> —DEUTERONOMY 28:15

Here in Deuteronomy, God gave Moses a two-item menu for the people to choose from for how they wanted to live. God said that they could choose to be blessed, or they could choose to be cursed. They could be above or beneath. They could loan to many, or they could borrow. They could prosper, or they could be poor. God even said, *"except when there may be no poor among you; for the Lord will greatly bless you in the land which the Lord your God is giving you to possess as an inheritance"* (Deut. 15:4).

God is against poverty for His people. God is also against sickness because *"He sent His word and healed them"* (Ps. 107:20). God said, *"I will take sickness away from the midst of you"* (Exod. 23:25). God gave us a choice. Do you want to be sick or well? Poor or rich?

Most people cannot handle wealth, which is why it evades them because it is where their focus is. Jesus said first seek God's face and His kingdom, and all of these other things will be added to you (see Matt. 6:33). The Word says that if you leave your family and houses and lands for His name's sake, you will receive in this life a hundredfold and inherit eternal life (see Matt. 19:29). Remember that with it come persecutions.

God set up the law to expose our inability to keep it. The Pharisees kept people captive so that they would have return customers. That is what satan does, and you can tell everything that he is involved in because you will never get a resolution on it. You keep going back for more advice, but you never get well. The whole system is set up in a corrupt way to keep you in a small place so that you keep coming back for more. But Jesus came to set you free—permanently free.

> *Therefore if the Son makes you free, you shall be free indeed.*
> —JOHN 8:36

God has set people in the church today who are now supposed to be guardians of the body of Christ. As a believer, you are supposed to be submitted to apostles, prophets, pastors, teachers, and evangelists. These fivefold ministers are responsible and accountable for the body of Christ. They are to bring resolution, and they are not here to keep you captive. They are not here to keep you needing another word, another book, or another DVD series.

You must come to a place where what Jesus said comes to pass, and that is God's way. God's ways lead you into freedom, and you should not need the things you previously needed anymore. The reason addictions happen is that we have not discerned what Christ has done for us. We have not been seated with Him in heavenly places even though we are.

Many Christians have been taught to focus on their problems and their needs. They have been told to give money to get money instead of learning how to receive from God. I give to God because I want to, and I know that it is for my benefit that I give. God does not need my money; He needs my fellowship and my time, and I give God my time, which is worth more than my money.

If I sow into healing, I can reap healing. I have to sow into healing, and I do not do that by giving money for my healing. You do not have to pay money to have that done. You cannot get into these kinds of things because it is where you will become bound again. You do not need to give any money to get healed, get a word, or sit in the front row. You can see how easily these kinds of things can become corrupt. If the guardians, the five-fold ministries, become corrupt, then what happens is the people get robbed. The people fall short because the system becomes corrupt, and it never brings resolution. I pray that you will have resolution and that you will not need me, but you have to rise up and be seated with Christ.

The Pharisees would never have had this kind of doctrine being taught in the synagogues because they would have no longer been needed. You no longer have to go to the priest or the pope to confess your sins because you can go to the one Mediator between God and man, which is Jesus Christ (see 1 Tim. 2:5). Once you realize that there is no other in-between besides Jesus, then the corrupt system is no longer needed. That corrupt system will get very angry, and that is what happened to Jesus.

> *To him who overcomes I will grant to sit with Me on My throne, as I also overcame and sat down with My Father on His throne.*
> —REVELATION 3:21

Jesus died on the cross and went down into the heart of the earth and was raised to life. He then went and sat at the right hand of God in the heavenly places (see Matt. 12:40; Eph. 1:20). Jesus took you and me with Him so that now it is a local call to the throne because you are seated with Him in the heavenly places. When I was in Heaven, I got to sit on the throne mentioned in the Book of Revelation (see Rev. 3:21). Jesus said that if you overcome and are victorious, you will sit with Him and the Father on His throne, and that is the truth.

All the angels cannot figure out why God looks at us and favors us. We have been placed higher than the angels, but it is not apparent now because of the fall. The angels have an advantage over us because we do not see into all the realms as they do. We can only see one-sixth of light, and our hearing is not as acute as before the fall. There are realms that are not open to us like they used to be before man fell. We have to become spiritually active through the born-again experience to tap into what is around us in the other five-sixths of the spectrum of light. It is about so much more than being able to appreciate the rainbow's beautiful colors. Some spectrums expose other realms that are hidden from our eyes.

Have you ever noticed that you can see movement around you out of the corner of your eye? You can see things, and it has to do with how light bends and how your eye is made. There are times that if you look straight ahead, you will see movement on either side of you. Those are God's angels and, hopefully, no demons. The spirit realm is wide open to us through Jesus Christ, and we only need to go to Him and be seated with Him.

You need to have an edge about you, a command about you, an authority knowing that mountains have to move if you tell them to move. You must be a "seated with Him in heavenly places" kind of Christian. The problem is that our world is so small because we have not allowed God to take the limitations off of us in our perceptions. They have already been taken off spiritually, but many of us go through life and never know this.

I realize the gift I have been given of getting to see this from the other side in Heaven and then being sent back. I want to tell you that all my years of study and all the degrees I have on my wall mean nothing to me now. They cannot compare to the one glimpse I saw of how vast God's kingdom is and how powerful it is. To see how loving and kind Jesus is and that He has nothing in Him to in any way hurt you, and that through His love He bought you at a price. Jesus has given us this age of grace that we are in right now to love people and try to help them.

When people go their own way, then judgment comes. If someone has not accepted Christ, they are not redeemed, and they are not walking in Jesus. They cannot walk in the blessings of God, and evil spirits can touch them. Then satan can take them over and do what he wants with them. If you *are* born again, satan cannot take you over because you are a child of God. The devil then tries to get *you* to hand parts of yourself over to him. You have authority over your body, mind, will, and emotions, and you have to give that authority to satan yourself.

You give that authority to satan when you give yourself over to alcohol, or adultery, or pornography, or any kind of evil thing that takes you away from God. All of satan's evil spirits are instructed to get people hooked on things to gain access to those human beings. It is not easy to get people possessed because of the light that is in this country. The United States was dedicated to God at one point, and now God wants His country back.

I saw that demons were instructed to get people hooked on something other than God to make it very hard for people to be impassioned for God. The last thing satan wants is Christians getting together singing and dancing and praying in tongues. It is okay to dance and shout and raise your hands at a ballgame, and that is why they moved professional sports from Saturday to Sunday. I saw that satan and his demons are trying to make it so that you are dumbed down and hooked on something other than God.

You do not go to hell because you smoke or have other bad habits. You go to hell because you have not accepted Jesus Christ as your Savior, or you have but you rejected Him. As a Christian, you can get to the place where a demon can get in and convince you that you do not need Jesus Christ anymore, and that is the unpardonable sin. When you tell Jesus that you do not want Him anymore, that is how your conscience becomes seared. If you have said something like that from a place of hurt and still have a conscience about it, you have not committed the unpardonable sin. The people who have meant it know what they are doing, and they do not care.

The demonic spirits want to get you away from God. Anything that causes you not to look at Jesus Christ and trust Him is a sin. When you sin, you need to repent. Repentance is when you turn back toward Jesus because something has taken your gaze away from Him. Your gaze is now on something else, and it is controlling you because you have handed yourself over to it. If you correctly adhere to God's ways, the limitations are taken off. If you had a revelation of how much God loves you and what He has for you, you would not have to sin.

This is the message which we have heard from Him and declare to you, that God is light and in Him is no darkness at all. If we say that we have fellowship with Him, and walk in darkness, we lie and do not practice the truth. But if we walk in the light as He is in the light, we have fellowship with one another, and the blood of Jesus Christ His Son cleanses us from all sin. If we say that we have no sin, we

*deceive ourselves, and the truth is not in us. If we
confess our sins, He is faithful and just to forgive us
our sins and to cleanse us from all unrighteousness.
If we say that we have not sinned, we make Him a
liar, and His word is not in us.*

—1 JOHN 1:5-10

The first Epistle of John is never quoted anymore. John talks about being in Christ and not sinning, but there is forgiveness for sin if we do sin. John goes on to say that whoever abides in Christ does not sin (see 1 John 3:4-9). Someone has to be brave enough to preach the whole Gospel and not be afraid. There is a place where we can walk with God, where we start to manifest His glory, and things start getting out of our way. That is the ultimate, for God. God's heart is that the Gospel would be preached and that people would be free, not just of sin, but free to walk with Him and love Him and know His heart.

*But Jesus didn't trust them, because he knew all
about people. No one needed to tell him about
human nature, for he knew what was in each person's heart.*

—JOHN 2:24-25 NLT

God wants to reveal His heart to us, but He does not just trust people because He knows what is in a man. John said here that Jesus never entrusted Himself to anyone because Jesus knew what was in a man. Jesus knew that man had a choking point, and he would sell out against Him. We all have our breaking point because of the weakness that is in our flesh. But what if

I told you that Jesus showed me that there is no one in Heaven limiting you at all? That is the truth. The devil knows he is going to lose you, so why not make it quick? You have got to stop dating him during the week and just fix your gaze on Jesus.

> *However, when He, the Spirit of truth, has come,*
> *He will guide you into all truth; for He will not*
> *speak on His own authority, but whatever He hears*
> *He will speak; and He will tell you things to come.*
> *He will glorify Me, for He will take of what is Mine*
> *and declare it to you. All things that the Father*
> *has are Mine. Therefore I said that He will take of*
> *Mine and declare it to you.*
> —JOHN 16:13-15

If you listen to someone speak for an hour and never mention Jesus, they just say God, then that is not the Holy Spirit ministering through that person. The Holy Spirit does not speak on His own authority, but as it says here in John, when He does speak, He will tell you things to come. The Holy Spirit will glorify Jesus, and He will take what was Jesus' and declare it to you. The Holy Spirit is only going to speak what He hears.

Well, guess what? Contrary to popular belief, you are not the subject of the Gospel message. If you talk about yourself for an hour, then all the people will get is you, not what the Spirit of God was sent to do. The Holy Spirit was sent to speak on the Father's behalf of the things to come and glorify Jesus and take what was Jesus' and make it known to you.

I saw that Jesus was sitting at a table, and it was the Last Supper communion table. Jesus was sharing these wonderful things with anyone who would come and dine with Him. I saw that the whole body of Christ is supposed to be coming and sitting with Him. You are not there to talk about yourself, but listen to what the Master has to say and let Him feed you. Let Him feed you at the table and partake of what He tells you to eat. Jesus will feed you from the implements, the bread, and the wine, which is His flesh and His blood.

In the Gospel of John 6:50-69, Jesus saw that many people were following Him, who were only spectators. He saw that they were following Him around because they had seen the miracles and were being fed. Jesus said, *"unless you eat the flesh of the Son of Man and drink His blood, you have no life in you"* (John 6:53). From that time, many of His disciples went back and no longer walked with Him. So they were only spectators.

Moses knew God's ways. Israel saw God's acts, but they watched them from a great distance (see Ps. 103:7). The Israelites never came up and had a relationship with God.

CALLED TO THRIVE

Many will say to Me in that day, "Lord, Lord, have we not prophesied in Your name, cast out demons in Your name, and done many wonders in Your name?" And then I will declare to them, "I never knew you; depart from Me, you who practice lawlessness!"

—MATTHEW 7:22-23

You cannot take this verse out of the Bible, and on that day Jesus is going to say this to many people. This verse is not going to go away because Jesus did not die so that you can go and live in an apartment in Heaven and not go to hell. Jesus died and redeemed you so that the Father can have you back in a relationship with Him. You are not just surviving down here; you are *thriving* in a relationship with your heavenly Father.

> *Jesus replied, "Loving me empowers you to obey my*
> *word. And my Father will love you so deeply that we*
> *will come to you and make you our dwelling place."*
> —JOHN 14:23 TPT

Some people read this Scripture and make a bedtime story out of it. It is such a nice feeling that perhaps God would come and live with them. Do you realize that mountains burned and melted like wax, and valleys split when God came and touched them? Do you realize that at the sound of His voice, the heavens thundered? Yet God has chosen Himself to live in you and to make His home in you. If you take this Scripture and add it to the fact that you will never be left as an orphan, you see that the Holy Spirit will come and live with you always (see John 14:15-18).

You are never going to be left alone again because the Spirit of Truth will be with you forever. Together, these verses show that the whole Holy Trinity is living inside of you, and you are not alone. You are not broken because God wants to heal you. Whatever it is that causes you to need addictions, God wants to fulfill that in you. There must come a tipping point where the

Gospel is preached, and there is a permanent change, and the problem never reoccurs again.

When I was in Heaven, I saw that Jesus was not going to defend Himself, and I saw that the Father was not going to defend Himself. It did not seem fair, and I was sad. I told Jesus that He was the most misunderstood person on the earth and the most misrepresented person. I looked at Jesus, and I could not believe that anyone would ever hurt Him. I saw that His beard had been restored, and everything about Him had been restored. He had beautiful skin, beautiful hair, nice three-foot-long hair, and lots of it. I could not believe that someone would pluck His beard out. In those 45 minutes that I was with Jesus, I could not understand why anyone would not like Him or why anyone would not receive Him. Jesus is irresistible, and when He talks you can see that He believes in every person, and He does not give up on them. Jesus empowers people, and He gives them a destiny.

To those who are turned from God who were predestined in Christ, Jesus keeps their destiny in Christ available for them. Their future is available until that person dies without receiving Him and goes to hell by their own choice. Jesus instructs the angels to keep them in a cycle of hearing the Gospel until they come to a place where they repent and turn to receive Jesus into their hearts and become born again. Unbelievers are continually sent to the Christians who will share the Gospel with them. The angels are sent and assigned to the unredeemed to bring them to someone who will preach and share the Gospel message with them. I saw this process happening in a continual cycle.

Angels are also assigned to Christians to cause them to yield and learn what they need to learn on a cyclical basis. However, it should not last for 40 years. If you have passed the same 7-Eleven several times, you are lost. The Israelites did that for 40 years, and no one was brave enough to say, "You know what? I think we passed this already because it looks familiar." They were in the wilderness of sin in a cycle that should have just taken them a couple of weeks to go through. It is time to take the limitations off.

I saw that satan has not only framed the way the world's system works, but once again he has inserted himself as a middle man in the church through religion. I will not make you feel good and send you away with a band-aid when you need surgery. On my watch, if you need surgery, you are going in because God needs to fix the problem at its root so that you are free. Jesus came to set you free, not to have recurring visits on the same subject (see John 8:36). There must come a time when there is a resolution. When the limitations are taken off, it causes you to go out into orbit instead of hanging around in the atmosphere's lower levels. You need to start enjoying your freedom in Christ and taking advantage of the benefits that God has given you.

STEP INTO OVERTHROW

There are times when someone calls you out at a service, and you get a word, or you get hands laid on you, and you feel the presence of God. You are required to go through a fire tunnel at some places, and there are all kinds of different carnival things that are out there. You may feel you are getting a breakthrough, but what you are mostly doing is experiencing someone else's environment.

The anointing is on that person ministering, and you do get a touch from God, but it is more often about that person having ministry gifts and anointing. That person has a walk with God, and you come under it, but once that person leaves your environment, you have to walk in it yourself. However, you can't walk in that because it took years for that person to learn how to walk in it themselves. You experience temporary freedom, but I suspect that those days are over; at least for me they are.

Jesus told me that He wanted transformation, which is a permanent change. I saw that we were supposed to be translated from the kingdom of darkness into the kingdom of light, which means there are no shadows anymore. You are on fire because you are seated with Christ, and you are taking commands from your Commander, who is also the head of angel armies. Jesus has heavenly angels at His disposal, and they do not take no for an answer. They know they can win. They know they can accomplish what God has told them to come and accomplish because God does not lie to them. God's angels have hearkened unto His voice, and they do His bidding. His angels and His ministers are flames of fire (see Heb. 1:7-9).

You need to move into overthrow, not just breakthrough, because overthrow is permanent. It becomes your domain, causing the devil to blink because he does not know what just happened. He has to pull the security tapes to see what just happened because there was a big flash. The devil remembers some sort of angel, and the next thing he knows he is on his back with a sword to his throat. A second ago, satan remembers he had a sword to your throat, and that is called overthrow. When you take dominion, it causes reversal, and then you are the one who is calling the shots.

I have waited patiently for years to tell you that the Jesus I met is into overthrow. I do not want another touch or another word. I want Jesus, and I want every devil in hell to know I got Him. Someone is going into overthrow! There have been so many generations that have gone on to Heaven before us. They have done their part because they were into overthrow, and they were not just into a breakthrough. They wanted to establish a foundation, and they were looking for a city whose builder and maker was God (see Heb. 11:9-10). They endured, looking to Him who is invisible (see Heb. 11:27).

These generations that came before were able to obtain the title deeds to their faith. They had substance inside them, even though they never got to see what we see today, but that did not stop them from building upon it. Now they depend upon us to build upon the foundation that they have already laid. We are not to rip it up and build our own, but we are to reestablish territories, re-dig the ancient wells, or sometimes simply sweep the dirt off the foundation. You do not need to build another foundation (see 1 Cor. 3:11-15).

Some people re-invent their ministry with a message that is just another message that has already been established, and they try to make it theirs. Well, it was never theirs. Solomon said that there is nothing new under the sun (see Eccles. 1:9). There are many voices, but there is none that is insignificant. They all have an origin, but there is only One who has spoken over you. There is only One who sings songs of deliverance over you and wrote a book about you. God Almighty is the One—this enforcer of the blessing who will make sure your book in Heaven is fulfilled if you learn to yield. You will only learn to yield if you acknowledge that the limitations have been taken off of you.

I am not going to reestablish a position that I already have. I will not take back the territory that someone else has already died for, which means I will not struggle in this life. I am walking on serpents and scorpions because Jesus said that is what you are going to do in His name. You need to hear some crunching under your feet. If you are really, truly a Christian, you need to adhere to what Jesus said. Christians adhere to the Master's voice, and they yield to the angels, and they let them do their job. It is a good thing when you wake up in the morning and you tell God's angels that you fully intend to cooperate with their assignment.

> *God sends angels with special orders to protect you wherever you go, defending you from all harm. If you walk into a trap, they'll be there for you and keep you from stumbling.*
> —PSALM 91:11-12 TPT

Angels have already been assigned with special orders concerning you, and that is why they are coming into your life. Joshua was by Jericho and got a little bit tense when he saw a soldier come with a drawn sword and stand in the middle of the road (see Josh. 5:13). Joshua was ready to fight anyone he perceived as a threat to the children of Israel. Moses had already died, and Joshua had been chosen to lead them into the Promised Land. Joshua went up to the soldier and asked, "Are you for us, or are you against us?" The angel said, "Neither, but as the Commander of the Lord's Army, I have now come." That is the kind of angel I have met. They do not give you their opinion because they are under orders from Heaven. Many angels did profound acts in the Bible, and we have never heard their names.

TAKE ON YOUR ASSIGNMENT

What is it that is hindering you? That giant needs to be taken out by you, and that is your assignment. The reason the demons come after you is that you have been destined to take them out. David found out that the giant Goliath was taunting Israel (see 1 Sam. 17:26). David was anointed to be king when he was younger by the prophet Samuel, but it would be many years before he would become king (see 1 Sam. 16:13). When David arrived at the battle scene where the Philistines and their champion Goliath were, he started asking questions. David could not figure out why the Israelite soldiers were not fighting and why King Saul had not given the command to take Goliath out. David's assignment became very clear to him, and he knew he would have to take out the giant because the established authority would not.

What happens when a five-year-old starts doing what the apostles are supposed to do? You will not even know what to think when a five-year-old is doing more than the established apostle. What if all Christians start doing what the apostles should be doing? Suddenly, the body of Christ will go into this next phase where the true apostles, the true prophets, the true pastors and teachers and evangelists arise because a five-year-old raised the bar. That is about to happen, and it is not too far away.

I saw in the Spirit that kids would take over, and they do not care if you call them apostles or not. They are not going to care, and they will not even want an offering. They will just want a popsicle or popcorn when it is all done.

The enemy wants to take out the whole generation that is in the womb right now. He has suspected that if Israel became a nation in 1948, the generation living during that time would be the generation that would have the *John the Baptist anointing* and the *Spirit of Elijah* on them. They would be the generation to proclaim the second coming of the Lord. So satan knows that there are deliverers in the womb, and that is why the prophetic voice is being taken out through abortion, and you are paying for it.

That is what satan did every time there was a deliverer in the womb. He did it through Pharaoh when he caught wind that a deliverer was coming, who was Moses, and he took out all the babies. When Jesus was born, the magi told King Herod of Jesus' prophecy, and satan again caught wind that there was a deliverer in the womb. The enemy, through Herod, put to death all the male children under two years old in Bethlehem and surrounding areas. Despite all this, satan missed Jesus, he missed Moses, and now he will miss the prophets and the prophetesses in the womb.

You look now at the generation that is coming up because they will proclaim the coming of the Lord. We have been bought time, so many people will have to throw away their end-time DVDs. They are right in their theology, but they are wrong in their timing because the timing depends on you. We are the ones who have to bring in the harvest, but we have to do it in power.

The only reason that God gave us that power is so that it could provoke people to jealousy.

"All these blessings shall come upon you and overtake you, because you obey the voice of the Lord your God" (Deut. 28:2). If they chose the Lord their God that day and did what He told them, then all of His blessings would come upon them. *"Then all peoples of the earth shall see that you are called by the name of the Lord, and they shall be afraid of you"* (Deut. 28:10). God said this to establish His covenant with them so that all the nations would see that He was the true God and that He blessed His people. Don't you think that the new covenant through Jesus Christ should fulfill all of that as well? God does not change personalities because there is a blank page between the Old Testament and the New Testament. He is still the same God, but it is just a deeper revelation.

If you do not believe in tithing, then just give 50 percent of your income. Please do not tell me about Old Testament Scriptures because Jesus did not have any New Testament Scriptures because He *was* the New Testament. Jesus was writing the New Testament, but He used Old Testament Scriptures. The apostle Paul used Old Testament Scriptures because there was no New Testament because he was writing it. So rip out the blank page and stop worshiping it because this is not the time to hide behind the blank page. You are free, and you give because you want to and not out of compulsion. You give so that it can be laid up to your account. You are free.

"Bring all the tithes into the storehouse, that there may be food in My house, and try Me now in this,"

says the Lord of hosts, "if I will not open for you the windows of heaven and pour out for you such blessing that there will not be room enough to receive it. And I will rebuke the devourer for your sakes, so that he will not destroy the fruit of your ground, nor shall the vine fail to bear fruit for you in the field," says the Lord of hosts; "and all nations will call you blessed, for you will be a delightful land," says the Lord of hosts.

—MALACHI 3:10-12

I do not see any other guarantee as I do here in Malachi regarding tithing. The devil just keeps walking because he sees that he is being rebuked. The devourer is rebuked for your sake if you tithe—again, if you do not believe in tithing, give 50 percent. My wife and I give more than that sometimes. You take a portion of what God has blessed you with, and you give it back to God, and it sets apart the whole. Then the devourer is rebuked, and the windows of Heaven are opened up so that you cannot contain what is about to be poured out on you. I do not see anything better than that.

However, do not be limited to the tithe only because we are in the New Testament now. It is probably at least 50 percent, and, in fact, it is all that you have. But you know what? Who's counting? When you get drunk on the new wine, it is just numbers. When I was in Heaven, I saw that nothing is mine, not even my body, and not my life. Jesus had possessed me and wanted to live His life out through me. At that time, there were only a few preachers who were preaching like that. These crazy people preached the real Gospel, and they have all gone to Heaven now.

R.W Shambach would say, "You know what, why don't you just swing out over hell and spit the devil in the eye." Dear Lord, you do not hear that stuff anymore. Can you imagine some of these mega-churches saying that today? You do not want to mess with the devil because you might lose your mega-church? Do you think the devil will come at you? Now think about that. Do you back off because of fear? Did God give you that church or not? In Heaven, there are so many saints who built upon what we enjoy today, and they died for what they believed. You enjoy the freedom of that, but you did not have to suffer as they did. Their accomplishments enabled the full Gospel to go forth and to be participated in and preached.

> *Who shall separate us from the love of Christ? Shall tribulation, or distress, or persecution, or famine, or nakedness, or peril, or sword? As it is written: "For Your sake we are killed all day long; we are accounted as sheep for the slaughter." Yet in all these things we are more than conquerors through Him who loved us. For I am persuaded that neither death nor life, nor angels nor principalities nor powers, nor things present nor things to come, nor height nor depth, nor any other created thing, shall be able to separate us from the love of God which is in Christ Jesus our Lord.*
> —ROMANS 8:35-39

THE POTENCY OF GOD

If you want to see the power of God and you want to see the limits taken off your life, then you will have to make an adjustment. You are going to have to take the full dose that is on the bottle, which means you are going to have to be a crazy friend. You are going to have to be able to pray all night if God tells you to. You are going to have to walk away from a meal. You have to be able to walk away from your best friend. The thing about it is, when you do that, you are going to experience such an overflow in your life because God is that potent. God is powerless in people's lives because they have not taken steps to go in through the narrow way. Once you are on the other side, you are going to see the mountain on fire. You are going to see the sapphire stones and the fire from the altar. You are going to experience these things and live in them every day.

However, you must remember what Paul said, *"But put on the Lord Jesus Christ, and make no provision for the flesh, to fulfill its lusts"* (Rom. 13:14). Paul further said, *"From now on, we regard no one according to the flesh. Even though we have known Christ according to the flesh, yet now we know Him thus no longer"* (2 Cor. 5:16). Paul went on to say that we know Christ now as seated at the right hand of God in full authority. Jesus is there waiting for His enemies to be made His footstool through the church—through you, the body (see Heb. 10:12-13). While you are waiting on Him, He has been waiting on you. It is time to take dominion and rule and reign.

Then Jesus said, "Father, forgive them, for they do not know what they do." And they divided His garments and cast lots.
—LUKE 23:34

The people did not discern who Jesus was. They were only concerned about the garments that He had on, and they divided them amongst themselves. While they were doing that, Jesus asked the Father to forgive them. Do you want to know why? It was because Jesus did not want anyone to go to hell. He did not want anyone to be in eternal damnation. Jesus told me that He and the Father never intended for anyone to go to hell. He said that hell was prepared for the devil and his angels, and no man was ever supposed to go there (see Matt. 25:41). No matter how much you dislike someone, you would never want them to go to hell. You should never want anyone to go to hell. What you want to do is drive the devil out. You want to keep him on the run, and you want *him* to go to hell because that is the devil's home; that is his destination. That is why hell was made for the devil and his angels, according to Jesus.

Or do you not know that your body is the temple of the Holy Spirit who is in you, whom you have from God, and you are not your own? For you were bought at a price; therefore glorify God in your body and in your spirit, which are God's.
—1 CORINTHIANS 6:19-20

This verse truly means that your life is not your own. It never was, because you were bought with a price. So you need to glorify

God in your body. You need to understand that your temple is your body and that the Lord dwells in it and that He wants your mouth, He wants your mind, and you do not have to be addicted to things. You have been bought with a price; therefore, glorify God in your body and in your spirit, which is God's.

> *Therefore, brethren, having boldness to enter the Holiest by the blood of Jesus, by a new and living way which He consecrated for us, through the veil, that is, His flesh, and having a High Priest over the house of God, let us draw near with a true heart in full assurance of faith, having our hearts sprinkled from an evil conscience and our bodies washed with pure water.*
> —HEBREWS 10:19-22

Jesus made a new and living way for us so that through His body, His name, and His authority, we are able to enter into the Holy of Holies. Then our bodies and our evil consciences are washed with His blood, and our bodies are washed and purified with the washing of the Word.

YOU ARE A DISTRIBUTION CENTER

Your world is small because *me, myself, and I* live there. You have to get to the place where your desires are God's desires and where He leads you into the deeper things that cause you to turn outward. God will fully support your getting there. Then you become a giver, and you help other people, and you do things for people who cannot pay you back. You begin to do things in secret because you have become a distribution center, and God will keep restoring your supply. You have to turn outward because the limits are taken off.

You cannot fail if you give your time to God. You must sow it even when you do not have it by giving people time when you do not have the time. Just do what God is telling you to do. You must start to turn outward and discern what God is saying to you and start helping people. Go out, preach the Gospel, and do it in a way where disciples are created, and that is what this is about; it is about creating disciples. Do not let *me, myself, and I* rule and reign anymore. Let God's flow go outward, and God will think about you when you don't think about yourself.

There has to be a shift in your perception, and the only way you can get that shift is to allow your spiritual eyes to be opened and see that you are seated with Christ. I had it happen to me, and I felt uncomfortable at first because Jesus was on my left hand, and He was at the right hand of God. The Father was at Jesus' left hand. As I looked down the row there to my left, I looked at Jesus, but I could see the Father. Father God was very big, but He was young. I could tell that He was young, but I was not allowed to look at His face. Jesus told me that if I saw the Father's face, my body would not take my spirit back because it could not handle what I just saw.

Jesus said that if my spirit beheld the Father, something would happen inside of my spirit. My spirit would not allow my body to live if my spirit went back and touched it because my earthly body was fallen. That is why your fallen body stays here on earth when you die. If you see the face of God, you cannot live in this earthly body. That is why Moses was not allowed to see God's face because he still had some work to do here before he could come and be with the Father. We cannot see God's face, but let us get as close to God as we can while we are here, and let's let Him have His way.

The Father recently had me watch space shuttle launches. In one, there were all these men and women all stacked in there. I think there were five or six people, and they were stacked laying back, standing straight up on the launch pad. They were told to put their visors down, and they were all strapped in, and suddenly they were going through the countdown. The ignition happened a couple of seconds before they were released. They have a hold on the shuttle to build up the thrust, and then they let it go. That is why you see all that fire. When they came off of that pad and start upward, they do all these procedures, and it has to be done in sequence.

I saw within just a short amount of time that the shuttle was in orbit. When they got out of the earth's atmosphere, everything became calm, and they were told they could take their visors off. They pulled them up, and they were in space, and they were high-fiving each other. I saw how much they had to fight against the earth to be weightless, to overcome the limitations. When the shuttle got into space, they went into orbit. They had accomplished that big task of overcoming the earth's gravity, and I saw that it took a lot of power to do that. When they did everything correctly, the shuttle made it into orbit.

I accidentally watched another launch from around the time when I was in college. I never knew that there was a launch that never quite made it into orbit, and they had to abort. One of the center engines went out, and they had to abort and come back and land at Edwards Air Force Base. I saw that there was not enough thrust to put them into orbit, so they came back in. In a short time, they were clear across the country already, and they came into California to land even though they took off from down in Florida. There wasn't enough thrust, and they did not escape the earth's atmosphere because the gravity was limiting them.

I saw that the same power that raised Jesus from the dead is dwelling in you, and it will quicken your mortal body (see Rom. 8:11 KJV). It causes you to overcome the things that are against you so that nothing can separate you from the love of God because perfect love drives out fear (see Rom. 8:35-39; 1 John 4:18). Nothing is left except you and God, and when He shows up He is perfect love. I saw that the power of the Holy Spirit is what has been given to us to take the limitations off. Not only does the Holy Spirit announce that your limits are off, but there is therefore now no condemnation, no record, no file, no accusing voice against you (see Rom. 8:1-2). The price has been paid, and you are free! Paul warns us not to entangle ourselves again in sin (see Gal. 5:1). We are not to take advantage of God's grace by sinning more so that grace would be revealed more. You are getting to the place where you do not want to sin because it is not fulfilling to you, and you realize that it is just delaying the overthrow.

Chapter 2

WALKING IN FORGIVENESS

And whenever you stand praying, if you have anything against anyone, forgive him, that your Father in heaven may also forgive you your trespasses. But if you do not forgive, neither will your Father in heaven forgive your trespasses.

—MARK 11:25-26

JESUS HAS TAKEN off the limitations through His blood, and we have free access into the Holy of Holies. However, we must forgive, and it is to *your* benefit to forgive. Jesus told me that it is to your benefit when you forgive people because it unhooks you from the curse. Forgiving someone does not mean that they get away with it. It only means that you can walk away from it, and it is *you* who gets away. Forgiveness is coming back into the body of Christ, and it is going to become popular to forgive people again. Either you will forgive, or your life is going to be cut short.

In this time that we live in, there will be a lot of offense that you will have to sort through, and you will have to let go of it every time. Jesus does not want you to get hooked by satan or in any way hindered from the glory because the glory is going to be very strong. You cannot be offended in the glory, and the move of God that is coming at you cannot be anchored down or tied up in any way. When God starts to move in His glory, He wants people to respond and work with Him, and you will have to have compassion for people.

Jesus could have been offended all the time, especially with His disciples, whom He was investing everything in. Jesus constantly had to explain things to them. You can tell how Jesus felt when He asked, "How long will I be with you?" (see Matt. 17:17). Jesus knew that He only had a certain amount of time to impart things to His people, and He was preparing them to carry on His ministry after He left.

When I was in Heaven, I saw how mistreated Jesus had been, and I realize now that if anyone should have been offended, it should have been Him. Yet Jesus said, *"Father, forgive them; for they know not what they do"* (Luke 23:34 KJV). Jesus could see the demons in the soldiers and all the people who came at Him. The Pharisees did not discern the day of their visitation and did not understand what was going on at the time. Jesus forgave them too, but He did not let them get away with anything. You have to forgive because you have got to free yourself up. The demons are very good at setting things up for you to be offended.

> *For assuredly, I say to you, whoever says to this mountain, "Be removed and be cast into the sea," and does not doubt in his heart, but believes that those things he says will be done, he will have whatever he says. Therefore I say to you, whatever things you ask when you pray, believe that you receive them, and you will have them.*
>
> —MARK 11:23-24

> *And whenever you stand praying, if you have anything against anyone, forgive him, that your Father in heaven may also forgive you your trespasses. But if you do not forgive, neither will your Father in heaven forgive your trespasses.*
>
> —MARK 11:25-26

I believe the most powerful thing that was ever spoken was what Jesus said in Mark 11:23 and 24. Jesus showed me that this verse had to do with Genesis 1:26 and how we were made in the image of God. We were the only species created that was like Him, and we were made in God's image. When you are born again and speak, you have spiritual power inside of you that forms in your words. That is why God has given you prayer, prophecy, tongues, and all the speaking gifts.

When you speak to a mountain, it will be removed because you believe in your spirit, not your head. When you believe in your heart, there is an ability spiritually that transfers into something physical, and you can see things move. Now, I am not talking about moving objects on a table. I am talking about spiritual entities that are in your way, things that are causing mountains to be in your way. Anything that is in your way of doing the will of God is a mountain.

Jesus told me that there was a reason that He put Mark 11:25-26 after Mark 11:23-24. For mountains to move, you cannot be holding offenses or walking in unforgiveness; that was why He put it there after speaking to the mountains. I believe that the reason mountains are not flying away is that people are in unforgiveness because Jesus put that verse right after that. After I was on the other side and looked back, I could see things without hindrance. I understood why Jesus talked about unforgiveness there because it is going to be a hindrance to you if you do not walk in forgiveness. You have to let go and free yourself up.

I could tell you stories of when I forgave people and how the people who did things to me did not get away with it at all. It is amazing to see what happens when you hand your case, with all of your files, over to your lawyer, your advocate, the Holy Spirit. That is when Jesus takes your case, and the whole court is rigged because His Father is the judge, and Jesus hands it over to the Father. Trust me, if you stay out of it and just listen to what your lawyer says to you, which is, "Do not say a word, just sit there and be quiet and I will talk for you"—that is a good lawyer.

I remember Kathi and I got a call from a friend in a church. He said, "You know, I have had it with your vehicle." I said, "You've never even driven it." He said, "Well, it is just so old. Meet me over at the Nissan dealership. We are gonna get you a new vehicle today." He was a car dealer for Bentleys and Porsches, but I just wanted a Nissan Pathfinder. He told me to meet him behind the building in the fleet department.

When I got there, my friend was sitting there talking with this guy. He was saying, "Oh, you are not gonna do this to him," and, "Take that off. No, you are not gonna do that either." The guy that my friend was talking to looked at me and said, "I can't get away with anything with your friend here because he knows all my tricks." I was thinking, *That is good. I have an advocate.* So I started to talk, and my friend turned to me and said, "Shut up, you are ruining the deal." I stopped talking, and we got a Pathfinder very inexpensively. It is now 19 years old, with 89 thousand miles on it. My mechanic says they have never seen anything like this car.

TESTING YOUR CIRCUMSTANCES

The thief does not come except to steal, and to kill, and to destroy. I have come that they may have life, and that they may have it more abundantly.
—JOHN 10:10

This verse shows you how you can test to see if God is in it or if the devil is in it. Every time something happens to me, I place this test of the Scripture on it. If someone or something is trying to kill me or steal from me or destroy me, I know it is the devil. If I have life more abundantly, I know it is God. How hard can that be? Jesus was speaking this to very simple people, and He was telling them the way it was.

Jesus represents abundant life, and every time I have encountered Jesus, I have encountered abundant life. I have encountered words that I can hang on to. I look at Jesus, and He is such a beautiful person, but He has fire in His eyes. Jesus appeared to me one time, and He pointed at me and said, "Do not find yourself on the wrong side of Me."

Another time Jesus appeared to me, He said, "I am the door." Kathi was asleep, and Jesus was standing at the foot of the bed. That was how I woke up, with Jesus standing there looking at me with fire in His eyes. I said, "Yes, I know You are the door. You said that in the Book of John." Jesus said, "Well, you do not understand obviously. You do not go anywhere on this earth unless it is through Me." Then Jesus turned around mad and walked out.

I had accepted an invitation to speak at a church without praying about it. It was my first invitation. When I was in college, my president said, "If you ever get an invite, take it because it will be a while before you can turn them away." I accepted the invitation, but I did not know that I would offend the Head of the church. Jesus was upset that I had not prayed before accepting the invitation. I have since gone back to that church to speak, but I learned my lesson well after that.

Jesus has appeared to me several different times when there was another side to Him. Jesus has a two-edged sword—one side is to cut me, and the other side is to cut my enemy. The Sword of the Spirit separates between your soul and your spirit (see Heb. 4:12). This sword shows you what is you and what is God. It pierces, and it is the only thing that will separate your soul from your spirit. You cannot tell the voice of your spirit from your soul until you allow the Word of God to come in and start separating. If you are in unforgiveness and the Lord tells you that, then that is the way it is. You must let that sword separate, and you must separate yourself from unforgiveness.

> *Then He said to the disciples, "It is impossible that no offenses should come, but woe to him through whom they do come! It would be better for him if a millstone were hung around his neck, and he were thrown into the sea, than that he should offend one of these little ones. Take heed to yourselves. If your brother sins against you, rebuke him; and if he repents, forgive him. And if he sins against you seven times in a day, and seven times in a day returns to you, saying, 'I repent,' you shall forgive him."*
>
> —LUKE 17:1-4

Woe to the one whom the offense comes through. If you are a child of God, you are one of the little ones, and God understands the pressure you are under on earth. If someone trips you up and causes you to sin, it would be better that they had a millstone tied around their neck than to trip you up. It says here that offenses are going to come, but woe to him through whom they come. It would be better for him if a millstone were hung around his neck.

I am trying to get you unhooked. You truly need to forgive and let God's justice system work. Trust me, because He will get in touch with you, and you will not have to call Him. God is going to take care of everything. I have already seen what God has for people who love Him, fear Him, and walk before Him. God does not withhold any good thing from those who walk uprightly before Him (see Ps. 84:11). So you need to forgive.

> *For if we would judge ourselves, we would not be judged. But when we are judged, we are chastened by the Lord, that we may not be condemned with the world.*
> —1 CORINTHIANS 11:31-32

Part of our life down here on this earth is being separate from the world. We are to stand out and be separate from among the people of the world. If you judge yourself, then you will not be judged with the world. When we are judged, we are chastened by the Lord. Can you believe this Scripture in the age of extreme grace? "But God loves me just the way I am." No, He does not. What a foul, lying devil that started that whole doctrine of extreme grace. "We can do anything we want." No, you cannot.

Extreme grace is this—Jesus says to you, "I love you, but if I want your opinion, I will give it to you." He is not asking for your opinion. He is going to tell you what your opinion is. Jesus is going to tell you, "This is the way to go; walk in it this way. I have a plan for your life. You are going to overcome the devil because I am going to route you around all the traps." Jesus knows that if you are left to yourself even for one minute, you will fall right into a trap because you are already in pride. That is one big trap, right there, and there is a fall coming. Pride comes before a fall (see Prov. 16:18).

You do not want to get into the trap of the devil, so you must judge yourself. You let the Spirit of God come in and separate between your spirit and your soul, which is your mind, will, and emotions. The Spirit of God will come in, separate, and tell you everything the way it really is, the reality of it all. Let the Holy Spirit do extraordinary things in your life, but for that to happen, you have to stay unhindered.

Let God's Word start to sprout and create a crop. When it does, you will not even understand what has happened to you. You will start to encounter demons, and you will have an attitude toward them. Something inside of you, called fire, will start to rise up, and you will start to address demons as you have never addressed them before. You will know when things are not right, and you will say, "Oh, no, we are not going to have it this way, not on my shift. I am going to call it as it is."

That is what happens when you have produced a crop from the Word that was sown into you, and it is permanent. God is giving you the ability to walk out this life, and the Spirit of God is going to start to fill in all the blanks. He is going to start to show you the things that are going on. You will start to understand, and you will realize that this world is messed up, but you are not because you have separated yourself from the world.

Coming out from among the world means that you do not want to be attached to the things of the world and its people. You judge yourself and let God chasten you if you need to be. *"Whom the Lord loves He chastens"* (Heb. 12:6). That is how the Father treats you and disciplines you as a son or daughter. You move out into this place that might seem lonely at times, but it is a very, very good place. It is a place where the boundaries have fallen in pleasant places for you, and you start to prosper in everything you do (see Ps. 16:6). God blesses those who follow His ways. He loves you.

ENFORCE THE WORKS OF GOD

He who sins is of the devil, for the devil has sinned from the beginning. For this purpose the Son of God was manifested, that He might destroy the works of the devil. Whoever has been born of God does not sin, for His seed remains in him; and he cannot sin, because he has been born of God. In this the children of God and the children of the devil are manifest: Whoever does not practice righteousness is not of God, nor is he who does not love his brother.

—1 JOHN 3:8-10

As children of God, we now know what we are supposed to do. We are ambassadors representing Jesus Christ. We must enforce what Jesus has already done, and He destroyed the works of the devil. Your job is to enforce that destruction, and you have to trip satan up and not let him rest. All of these evil spirits here on earth are disembodied spirits from the hybrids who lived before the flood. They want to stay in their location where they were before the flood. They are mad because there is no redemption for hybrids.

Jesus came back as a pure human being. All of the genealogies through the Bible confirm that no Nephilim had any influence on His family line. Jesus was the unblemished Lamb of God, and He was spotless. Jesus was perfect in His generations, just like Noah was. When Noah went on the ark with his family, there were only eight people in total on the ark. That was all because no one else qualified to go. Everyone else on the earth died in the flood. All the people who lost their bodies in the flood are now entities that roam the earth. They are angry, and they could care less about you. These disembodied spirits are mad because you are in, and they are out.

There is a whole other world around you, and the only reason you make a difference is that you adhere to the teachings of Jesus Christ. When you believe in Jesus Christ as your Lord and Savior, something happens in your spirit, and it is called faith. That faith, that trust in God ignites your heart to move and live and have your being in Him, and you have a command about you. When that happens, you need to stop being weak toward the devil. I do not know where we got the idea that humility is a weakness. Jesus was humble, but He was not weak.

> *Now the works of the flesh are evident, which are: adultery, fornication, uncleanness, lewdness, idolatry, sorcery, hatred, contentions, jealousies, outbursts of wrath, selfish ambitions, dissensions, heresies, envy, murders, drunkenness, revelries, and the like; of which I tell you beforehand, just as I also*

told you in time past, that those who practice such
things will not inherit the kingdom of God.
—GALATIANS 5:19-21

Sorcery is involved in the works of the flesh, which is witch-craft. It is interesting to note that Paul lists witchcraft in the works of the flesh. Most people think that witchcraft is a spiritual thing. The apostle Paul was caught up, and he understood all of this. Paul said, *"The weapons of our warfare are not carnal but mighty in God for pulling down strongholds"* (2 Cor. 10:4). Paul goes on to say that you have to bring into captivity every thought to the obedience of Christ. Anything that exalts itself above the knowledge of God, you have to bring it into captivity, pulling it down, and *this* is spiritual warfare.

Why does Paul list sorcery or witchcraft as a work of the flesh? It is because those evil entities need your body. They need to have an expression on the earth, so they need your mouth, and they need to get into your mind to convince you, and then they move in. The degree that people hand themselves over to the demon is the degree to which the demon will get hold of them.

It is crazy to think that a Christian could do this, but they can hand parts of themselves over and manifest some of these things. It has to do with domains and dominion, and it does not have to do with possession. If you study the words out, the word there is *demonized* and has to do with domains, proximity, ownership, and rulership. Do not ever turn yourself over in any area of your life so that an evil entity can influence you in any way. Christians should not have anything to do with the devil at all, period.

You do not need to reverse engineer the stars to figure out what God is doing because you can ask Him. You are a child of God, and you can go in and get counsel from Father God through the Holy Spirit, and He will counsel you. You do not need to read astrology or inquire of any necromancer or any other evil spirit. Witches need to get saved and get rid of their familiar spirits.

Jesus showed me ministers who got lazy and they stopped moving, but God keeps moving. When these ministers were not producing because the giftings were not working, a familiar spirit came in. These ministers are 100 percent accurate, but I do not need to know my Social Security number because I already know it. I do not need to know my address or my mother's name. I already know them, so it does not impress me. I can sit in a service, and when it shifts I know this is a familiar spirit, and it is not God.

A true prophet will tell you the dream you had last night and then interpret it. These spirits will accommodate you if you let them, so you cannot stop moving with God. You have to stay in there with God. You do not know everything, but you can have discernment to look and see that something is not right and that it does not measure up. The Lord is trying to get people ready for the harvest.

When you get to Heaven a thousand years from now, the only thing that is going to count is what you did for Him. Everything that you sacrificed for the Lord, you will be repaid. It is out of my hands because I am laying up treasures in Heaven (see Matt. 6:19-21). You can also lay up treasures in Heaven when you do things for people who cannot pay you back, and you do it because you love God. Anything you give, you give it because you love

God. When you are not acting under compulsion, you do not worry about it. Let God speak to your heart about whatever you do and know that you cannot lose.

It is all about winning souls, winning people over, and convincing them that God is with you. People want to see the manifestation of God. They wanted to know why I was a Christian and how I could do what I was doing. They wanted an answer when I explained to them that on the other side of this physical world is another world, and *that* is the real world. I told them that Jesus came to buy God's family back. And everyone has a book written about them in Heaven, whether they live it out or not, whether they go to hell or not (see Ps. 139:16).

God has already written a book about everyone because He wants everyone to come to Heaven, so He lets people decide. It bothered me when I was in Heaven to see how much God loves people, and yet He is so misrepresented on this earth. God might have you do something that is what we would call unconventional. It might be something uncommon or out of the ordinary, but listen to me—you cannot lose. The limitations have been taken off.

You Cannot Lose

When the Son of Man comes in His glory, and all the holy angels with Him, then He will sit on the throne of His glory. All the nations will be gathered before Him, and He will separate them one from another, as a shepherd divides his sheep from the goats. And He will set the sheep on His right hand,

> *but the goats on the left. Then the King will say to those on His right hand, "Come, you blessed of My Father, inherit the kingdom prepared for you from the foundation of the world."*
>
> —MATTHEW 25:31-34

To understand me personally, you have to understand that I was at the end, and I was with all of you. I was with everyone who ever lived who inherited the kingdom because every one of these people repented of their sins, and they accepted Jesus. I do not understand how God judges people who have never heard the Gospel, so do not ask me. I do not understand any of that stuff, and I am glad it is not my job, so I do not judge anyone. However, I was there with the saints at the end of the age, and we were all singing the song of the redeemed and worshiping the Lamb who sat on the throne. I saw Jesus receiving the reward for His suffering.

If every one of us realized that we make it, we would come back and live this life full out, full throttle, with reckless abandonment, and a passion that we cannot lose. No matter what you do for God, you cannot lose. You know that I know what I am saying because I have been there, and we make it. Now come back from that and work it! Come back and say, you know what? This earth is mine because God has given it to me.

One day the kingdoms of this world will be transferred over to the kingdom of our God (see Rev. 11:15). We are going to inherit the earth because we are meek. We will be ambassadors, and we will enforce the kingdom of God on this earth with angels under us. That is the way it is. I already saw all this in Heaven, and I have no problem with it.

The problem that I have is it is amazing how religion has robbed us of the truth and that we focus on things that are not important. The important things are taking care of each other and guarding the assets of God. Guarding what God has given us on this earth through our testimony, and guarding our testimony so that the people of the world can see that we have the only true God.

When I was at work, people wanted to know if God was real, and I had to have a good answer. When I would explain to them about destiny and how their books were written in Heaven, without exception, people would start crying, and they would repent right there. I could see that my testimony was giving them hope. Everyone wants to know that there is a plan and purpose for their life and a destiny. Everyone wants to be loved, accepted, and to feel safe. Everyone, that is, except the devil.

When I saw what happened in the Garden and saw how we were before the fall, I realized why Jesus came back. We fell so far that we do not have a standard to measure how far we have fallen. When I was in Heaven, I had no hindrance from the curse. I had no hindrances at all; I did not fight myself, I did not doubt, and I had no fear. I knew my purpose, and I was happy. God was happy. Everyone was happy. I saw that was the way it was before the fall. However, down here on earth, there is a satanic kingdom. All of satan's evil spirits are bent on destroying God's creation and His kingdom. The demons want to destroy how you look at God and view everything. They want to demolish your entire world view.

My professor in college was an astronaut, and he also flew spy plane missions above the atmosphere. He told me that he would be up there in the airplane for 14 hours when he went on missions. When he came back into the earth's atmosphere, he said he could feel the demonic realm. He once told me that Neil Armstrong was a friend of his. Neil had told him that when he was on the moon, there were no demons there. There were no demonic forces there because there were no people there, and because of that Neil had no hindrances. Neil could hear God speak right back to him when he would have his devotions. God would answer him, and they would speak back and forth.

My professor told me that he had to stay high enough on missions so that the missiles couldn't hit him. He was flying over different countries and taking photos and things of that order. He said he was going five and a half times the speed of sound and being shot at, and the missiles could never reach him. He would just read his Bible and pray as the plane was on autopilot and just did its thing and outran the missiles. He said that he had a lot of stress, but he said the thing about it was that you could just be with God up there.

I have experienced that in the other realm at the throne room of God. Coming back down here is not so easy. You are constantly being confronted by demonic forces all the time. People have told me that there is no demon behind every tree, and I say they are right because there are five! It is easier to take the tree out to get rid of whatever they are hiding behind, and that is what I do. I just take out the tree and expose them, and that is what we are called to do because you cannot just cower and hide.

I beseech you therefore, brethren, by the mercies of God, that you present your bodies a living sacrifice, holy, acceptable to God, which is your reasonable service.

—ROMANS 12:1

Even though we are alive, we need to present our bodies on an altar because that is a sacrifice, but it is a living sacrifice. This sacrifice keeps your body in line by honoring God with your worship. Your body is the temple of the Holy Spirit, and you have to keep it in line. It is amazing that when I became a Christian, I did not know a lot of the things that I know now, and I am sure you feel the same way. You know more now than you did when you became a Christian.

However, if I would have known some of the things that I know now, I would have done so much better because I did not understand that my body does what it wants to do, and it does not like listening to me. I have to be able to tell my body, "No, you are not going to do that." I have to make a sacrifice and walk away from what I want. Something happens with your spirit when your body is presented on the altar, and it becomes stronger.

When I was in college in 1983, the Lord spoke to me and said, "I want you to fast two meals a day." I fasted then, and I am doing it again now, but it is not easy. However, when my work is done, my reward will be plenty. There will not be any meat in Heaven, but I will get to eat what I want except for the meat. The reason there is no meat is that there is no death. Very often, your body does not want to do what you need to do. Your spirit is trapped unless you train your mind to think a certain way. You must discipline and transform your mind by the Word of God.

Your spirit is so bright, and I know this because I got to see my spirit. I got to see several different things when I was in Heaven. I got to see the body that I get at the resurrection, which is different than the body I had while I was outside of my physical body in the operating room. I was wearing a robe of righteousness on my body in the operating room, and I was brightly shining. If that wasn't enough, Jesus gave me a preview of my glorified body, which is my resurrection body that I will not receive until the resurrection.

We are all going to look like God in the resurrection. The apostle Paul said, *"But we know that when He is revealed, we shall be like Him, for we shall see Him as He is"* (1 John 3:2). There is never going to be a time when you are any better spiritually than the born-again experience has already brought you to. You have been born again, and you are a new species—old things have passed away; behold, everything has become new (see 2 Cor. 5:17).

You can develop your spirit, and you can grow spiritually. However, you will not get any more holy than your spirit is right now because it has already become a new creature in Christ Jesus. This little thinking that we have is keeping us in a small place. Your body is the only thing that will not be redeemed until the resurrection. Your physical, earthly body is going to die, and it is not going to be redeemed. You will live a certain number of years, and then you will shed your earth suit and you will go to Heaven.

You can do things to keep yourself healthy and live longer, but death will come to everyone.

Your soul, which is your mind, will, and emotions, does not have to deteriorate. It can be redeemed, but it has to be transformed. Your soul can be saved, but your spirit is already saved. Your soul can be saved, but it must be renewed by the incorruptible, engrafted Word of God, and by doing that you cause your soul to side with your spirit. If your body is going to die, then you need to take care of it because it is the temple of the Holy Spirit. However, you need to concentrate on getting your soul (your mind, will, and emotions) to side with your spirit.

People of the Spirit

We must be people of the Word, but we have to be a people of the Spirit, too. The Word renews your mind. However, if you renew your mind and you do not yield to the Spirit of God, then it is not going to help you. You must allow the Spirit to move also. I was in a meeting where Brother Kenneth Hagin was speaking. He said, "We are known as a people of the Word, but there is a whole move of God that is going to be aborted if we do not become people of the Spirit." He said that not long before he died.

Your soul can become one with your spirit, but it is going to take some discipline. Your body, you are just going to have to tell it, "No, we are not going to do that right now." If you do not, your body will do what it wants and try to convince you of things that are not true. You have to correct your body and discipline it. Paul said, *"I discipline my body and bring it into subjection, lest, when I have preached to others, I myself should become disqualified"* (1

Cor. 9:27). No one is going to stop your body except you, and if you do not do it, next thing you know you are face down with handcuffs on because the law steps in. As Christians, we do not need to wait for the law to kick in because we walk in the law of love, which fulfills all the law. Now, I have just summed up the whole Bible.

You should spend all your time praying in the Spirit and building yourself up in the most holy of faith and keeping in the love of God (see Jude 1:20-21). Then you transform your mind with the Word of God by renewing it. You need to focus all of your time on getting your mind to side with spiritual things because a spiritual person makes judgments about all things (see 1 Cor. 2:15). I have just told you the process whereby you can walk in the Spirit of God, and you can see God profoundly move in your life.

In my life, I disagreed with some of the guidance that God gave me because it did not look like I would end up in the right place. I thought that I had to be a pilot because a pilot was very important, and also they made a lot of money. I was constantly being told to do things that kept me away from what I wanted to do. It is interesting, though, that the Lord had me become a flight attendant, which humbled me because I fought it. I had to apologize for the weather for 30 years and serve people Cokes and Sprite, and they were mad about that. I do not know how you can mess up Coke and Sprite, but I did somehow.

Suddenly, the company I was with started prospering, and they gave me stock every year. When I retired, I was a millionaire, and I did not do anything except show up for work. The baggage handlers made 12 dollars an hour, and they would retire with half a million just because they were there. If you are hooking up with what God has for you, then you do not know the potential that the Lord has hidden there. There is something hidden in why you are doing what you do, and you should just keep seeking the kingdom of God.

You are going to tell your body, "No, we are not going to do it that way" because God is telling you to do it this other way. You are going to tell your mind, "No, we are not going to think that because we would be placing an idol up in front of us, and we do not worship idols." Any vain imagination that you set up in front of you is idolatry. You can set something up, and it is not the truth. It might be a fact, but it is not the truth, and what you have done is placed your focus on something else other than Jesus Christ. When you do that, you will end up in a different destination than what God chose for you.

When people fall into sin, they always say, "I don't know how this happened." I know exactly how it happened because we are all human. It happened one step at a time. You do not just wake up and find yourself in sin because it is a process, and that has to be stopped in the body of Christ. I want us all to shine. To do that, you have to tell your body, "No, we are not going to do that. We are going to do Keto." You are going to tell your mind, "No, we are not going to think that way because God has already told me to go in this direction."

Every one of you is so important. Your value is through the roof. God placed things in you, and then He placed a demand for your gift that is through the roof. First, God places things in all of us, and then He places the demand for that gift around you. That is how you meet the needs of the people.

I prayed and asked God, "What is it that people need?" God told me, and I received 59 titles for books to write. All I am doing is meeting your needs and my needs because God wants to meet needs. If you want to start a business, just find out what people need. You can have guaranteed success when you meet people's needs.

When I was a flight attendant, my company president was on TV, and all the other airlines were mad because they said he was ruining their business by driving them out of markets. The president said, "I am not competing against you. I am competing against the car." That was why he created an airline to get people who drove and would not normally afford to fly. He changed the whole airline industry because he saw that there was a huge need. Only 40 percent of the people could afford to fly until Southwest Airlines came along. He caused everyone else in the industry to bring their fares down, and he did not stop there. I was on flights that people paid $19 for the flight. You can imagine what's happening if a minister starts giving things away. It changes everything. It causes everyone to have to rethink why they are doing what they are doing.

God is not mad at you. He just wants you to talk to Him. What did God tell Cain? God said, "Don't you know if you do right, you will be accepted?" (see Gen. 4:7). God came and pleaded with Cain. "Can we work this out?" And that is what the Father is saying right now by the Spirit of God.

Father, I just ask that we receive forgiveness right now. Father, love on us; Lord, we need Your love. We need to encounter You. Open us up, and increase our capacity to receive Your love right now in the name of Jesus.

Chapter 3

REPENTANCE IS A KEY

*Repent therefore and be converted, that your sins
may be blotted out, so that times of refreshing may
come from the presence of the Lord.*

—ACTS 3:19

I CAME BACK FROM Heaven with a deeper understanding of some of the church's basic teachings today, and repentance is one of them. There is an obvious meaning to repentance, as Jesus said, *"Repent, for the kingdom of heaven is at hand"* (Matt. 4:17). In other words, you do not want to go to hell, so you repent. However, Jesus told me that the most effective way to preach the Gospel is to reveal God's goodness, knowing that the goodness of God leads you to repentance (see Rom. 2:4).

Repentance to me was when I realized that something had caused me to look away from my mark, which is the high calling of God in Jesus Christ (see Phil. 3:14). Religion seems to make it something that is more about condemnation. That is where everyone is walking around with their head down, and they are feeling defeated. This attitude causes God's children to be ineffective in their generation because the religious system has so beaten them down.

Jesus explained to the Pharisees that He came to break the yokes off of the people, the ones that the Pharisees had put on the people of God. Jesus said to the Pharisees, *"Woe to you, scribes and Pharisees, hypocrites! For you travel land and sea to win one proselyte, and when he is won, you make him twice as much a son of hell as yourselves"* (Matt. 23:15). Jesus did not hold back on the Pharisees. He not only talked behind their backs, but He talked right to their faces.

I saw that Jesus is the kindest person, and if you misunderstand something, He only wants to convince you otherwise. However, there is also a part of Jesus that if you do not want to have any part of Him, then you are a brood of vipers as He told the Pharisees (see Matt. 23:33). When the Pharisees came out to His baptism, Jesus said to them, *"Brood of vipers! Who warned you to flee from the wrath to come?"* (Matt. 3:7). He had no mercy on them whatsoever. It is okay to be resistant and rise up against any type of religious thinking that takes away from God's power.

REVEALING GOD'S GOODNESS

Jesus came back to seek and save those who are lost, not throw them in hell (see Luke 19:10). Jesus does not throw anyone into hell, but they go to hell because they choose to go there. I have met people who think that there will be a party down there and that they will just continue to party. They better be praying for air conditioning because it is really hot down there. The religious system is going to take away from the power of God and try to twist things. The enemy knows that he cannot take away truth, so what he does is he twists the truth. In these last days, we are going to have to be very sharp.

I saw in Heaven that we need to reveal God's goodness. We need to let God walk before us as He did with Moses. God said to Moses, *"I will make all My goodness pass before you, and I will proclaim the name of the Lord before you"* (Exod. 33:19). Then God hid Moses in the cleft of the rock, and God covered him with His hand while His goodness passed by Moses. God took away His hand so that Moses could see God's back as He passed by. The revelation of God that Moses had from that cleft in the rock was enough for him to write Psalm 91.

When the goodness of God passed by Moses, God announced His name to Moses. Moses gave Aaron, the first High Priest in the Holy of Holies, God's name, which no one else knew. No one was allowed to speak that name out loud except the High Priest with the blood offering inside the Holy of Holies. Once a year, with the sprinkling of blood on the mercy seat on the day of atonement, the name of God would be pronounced. Aaron whispered it to the next High Priest, and it was passed on from generation to generation.

Religion will try to duplicate and replicate the things of God. Jesus was coming against the Pharisees, even though their origin came from God. The Pharisees were supposed to enforce Moses' law and oversee the people, and they were to be like judges. In John 10:34, Jesus tells the Pharisees that they are *Elohim*, to whom the Word of God had been given. The word Elohim actually can mean judges as well. The Pharisees were part of God's entourage in their inception, but they had gone rogue. God instituted the law through Moses to curb sin and help people do right because they would not do it on their own.

With the law, God also wanted to show that we could not fulfill the law and that its purpose was essentially to expose sin. Paul's writings talk about how the law was given so that we would know what sin was. Paul said that he was powerless to fulfill the law. The good things that Paul wanted to do he did not do and the evil that he did not want to do, he practiced (see Rom. 7:13-25). In other words, there was a struggle going on inside of Paul, and the law was not able to fulfill the righteous requirement. But now, through the Spirit, if we put to death the misdeeds of the body and live according to the Spirit, then we fulfill all the righteous requirements of God through the Spirit in Jesus Christ our Lord!

> *For if you live according to the flesh you will die; but if by the Spirit you put to death the deeds of the body, you will live.*
> —ROMANS 8:13

When Jesus was talking to the Pharisees, He was telling them that they were putting yokes on people. Jesus was essentially saying, "I have come to set people free, and I have the answers. I have come to take you back to the Father, but it is by the Spirit." Jesus told them that if you love God with all your heart and love your neighbor as yourself, you fulfill all the commandments (see Matt. 22:37-40). If you love God and love your neighbor as yourself, you will not do anything to violate people or God. You will fulfill everything.

> *For what the law could not do in that it was weak through the flesh, God did by sending His own Son in the likeness of sinful flesh, on account of sin: He condemned sin in the flesh, that the righteous requirement of the law might be fulfilled in us who do not walk according to the flesh but according to the Spirit.*
> —ROMANS 8:3-4

Jesus was the fulfillment of the law and gave us a shortcut: to love your neighbor as yourself and love the Lord your God with all your heart. When you live your life like that, you do not need a police officer with a radar gun because you think of other people who might not be watching out for themselves. You obey the laws, and you do everything necessary to honor other people.

When corruption comes into the law, we have what we are dealing with today, the swamp, and what happened to religion. Jesus told me not to focus on people's condition of sin. I do not even talk about certain sins, and I do not even talk about hell. I am not going there, and I don't even want to visit.

Turning Toward Jesus

I saw that this is a much deeper issue than what we have been taught religiously about repentance. If anything draws your attention away from God, even a ring or a little trinket, a car, anything that you stare at, you need to repent. However, repentance means you are just turning back around toward the mark, toward Jesus, and it is not a religious thing.

You may be craving to eat all the time. By backing off of that behavior, you are just bringing correction to something you are going through. You need to tell your body, "No, I am in charge here." You begin to live out of your spirit and out of the goodness of God. The goodness of God leads me to turn my face toward Him, and that is repentance. It is not, "Repent or you are going to hell." Not even John the Baptist spoke like that. He said, "Repent for the Kingdom of God is at hand" (see Matt. 3:2).

I have noticed a difference in a believer's walk with God based on how they came to the Lord. Some people have been told that they are going to hell unless they repent, and they come to the Lord because they do not want to go to hell. Other people are converted to the Lord. They convert because they have had a revelation of how good God is and His love for them. There is a difference in discipleship between these two types of people.

When I tell people about Jesus, I tell them about God's plans for people and the books written in Heaven about them. I tell them that they do not want to go to hell because God has plans for everyone, and no one is supposed to go to hell. I tell them that Jesus said that hell was made for the devil and his angels and not for man. I notice that people are much more powerful disciples when they have a revelation of the Father's love. People who have come in because of the fear of hell have no revelation of God's love. Without a revelation of the goodness of God, these believers spend the rest of their Christian life almost afraid of God.

I started to notice this because the Lord wants disciples. He is assigning me to make disciples, but I do not want to concentrate on the negative. I think people already know that what they have is not getting them anywhere. I also know a lot of Christians who are not going anywhere. Didn't Jesus say, "Produce fruit in keeping with repentance"? Remember that everything in this realm is designed to pull your attention away from God.

> *Therefore bear fruits worthy of repentance, and do not think to say to yourselves, "We have Abraham as our father." For I say to you that God is able to raise up children to Abraham from these stones. And even now the ax is laid to the root of the trees. Therefore every tree which does not bear good fruit is cut down and thrown into the fire.*
> —MATTHEW 3:8-10

Jesus was very consistent, and He knew that the Pharisees were always going to be the Pharisees. Jesus always had compassion for the people who were sick and hungry. Whenever the people yelled out, "Son of David, have mercy on me," they were healed. The key was *Son of David*, and when they yelled that out, they were discerning that Jesus was of the lineage of David and the Messiah. In essence, they were calling out, "Messiah, have mercy on me." They were discerning who Jesus was.

When Jesus went to Nazareth and they discerned Him as the carpenter's son, all they got was a table and chairs. They did not get healed there. They did not partake because they did not see who Jesus was, and they never discerned it. It says Jesus could only do minor works there and did not heal many people because of their unbelief (see Matt. 13:58).

Not understanding repentance can cause you to be robbed of your encounter with God in its fullest sense. Through disinformation, some people believe that they only need to repent once. They are being taught that they do not need to repent more than that. I am not the kind of person who likes to confront things, but Paul confronted things all the time. Paul was a true apostle because he was a father, but he was jealous over people because so many came in and tried to snatch away his people through false doctrine. Paul was a defender of the faith. As Paul told Timothy, you have to stand up for right doctrine (see 2 Tim. 4:2-4).

> *Then with meekness you'll be able to carefully enlighten those who argue with you so they can see God's gracious gift of repentance and be brought to the truth.*
>
> —2 TIMOTHY 2:25 TPT

Disinformation can cause us to be robbed of something very powerful. Repentance is one of the things that satan has infiltrated and uses to start to get us off track. Repentance is very potent, and we cannot let it be taken from us. Repentance is a gift. Did you know that? In this scripture, Paul referred to "God's gracious *gift* of repentance."

> *Repent therefore and be converted, that your sins*
> *may be blotted out, so that times of refreshing may*
> *come from the presence of the Lord.*
> —ACTS 3:19

When you turn back to God, when you turn around, it says that your sins will be removed. It does not say anything about going to hell. It sounds like the Gospel message. Turn back to God, and your sins will be removed, and times of refreshing will come and will stream from the Lord's presence. That is the message that you should present to people because they are true disciples when you get a convert this way.

They become true disciples because they discern their Father, God. They discern a loving God, and many people have never encountered an earthly father like that. When you realize that God has certain ways of doing things but you know that He is a good God, then you trust Him. You then get rid of these unrealistic expectations toward God because you know who He is.

UNREALISTIC EXPECTATIONS

Some of the disciples were zealots. Did you know that they were a secret assassin group? The zealots would try to isolate Roman soldiers, and they would kill them, and there were several of them among the disciples. Judas was one of them. If you remember, there was one zealot in the Bible who had tried an insurrection and failed and ended up in jail, and his name was Barabbas. The crowd chose to free Barabbas from prison over Jesus on the feast of Passover in Jerusalem (see Matt. 27:15-26).

In Israel, at the time of Jesus, they were experiencing an unrealistic expectation, which is not different than what we are experiencing in America right now. In Israel, they believed that a deliverer would arise who would drive Rome and its soldiers out of Israel. They thought the Messiah would be a physical king who would then take the throne in Jerusalem. On the day that Jesus made His triumphal entry into Jerusalem, the multitudes cried out, *"Hosanna to the Son of David! Blessed is He who comes in the name of the Lord!"* (Matt. 21:9). They were so excited when Jesus arrived, even though He did not announce Himself as King of Israel and had no plans to drive Rome out. Within 24 hours of Jesus entering Jerusalem, all those in the synagogue wanted to throw Jesus over the brow of a hill (see Luke 4:28-30). Why? They thought that Jesus was another insurrectionist like Barabbas.

Then satan devised a plan, which included Judas. If satan had ever discerned God's plan, he would never have done this. Judas had a weakness in him. At the last supper at the Lord's table, Judas did not discern the Lord's body, and he did not discern the disciples, and this was a sacred thing. Judas ate unworthily of the communion table with Jesus there, and as soon as Judas ate the bread, it says that satan entered into him (see John 13:27).

That was why Paul said, *"He who eats and drinks in an unworthy manner eats and drinks judgment to himself, not discerning the Lord's body. For this reason many are weak and sick among you, and many sleep"* (1 Cor. 11:29-30). Judas never discerned the Lord's body, and he ate in an unworthy manner at the Lord's table.

Judas did not discern Jesus' body, and he did not discern the body of believers—the disciples—and he affected them all. Once satan entered Judas, he decided to turn Jesus over, and then there was no repentance. Then Jesus said to him, "What you do, do quickly." So Judas got up and left, and that was why the people wanted Barabbas back. It was because of unrealistic expectations. If you are in repentance, you will not be able to live in unrealistic expectations for very long because the Spirit is a Spirit of truth, and He is going to lead you into all truth.

It is important to understand this because one of satan's lies at the end of the age is that you do not need to repent anymore. That can cause you to get off in the wrong direction, and then there are no checks and balances in your life, and you are on your own. You can have unrealistic expectations about what God is saying to you.

> *You say, "I am rich. I have everything I want. I don't need a thing!" And you don't realize that you are wretched and miserable and poor and blind and naked. So I advise you to buy gold from me—gold that has been purified by fire. Then you will be rich. Also buy white garments from me so you will not be shamed by your nakedness, and ointment for your eyes so you will be able to see.*
> —REVELATION 3:17-18 NLT

While on the Island of Patmos, Jesus had John write to the seven pastors because they were not listening (see Rev. 1:11). *"He who has an ear, let him hear what the Spirit says to the churches"* (Rev. 2:7). It should not have been that way. Those churches should have had a pastor who could hear from God. They should also have had a prophet to confirm what God was saying within the body. Jesus had come to the Laodicean church to tell them that they did not discern their condition. Do you understand that was because they had a lack of repentance? They had a lack of focus on Jesus.

As long as I walk with the Lord, I do not need someone to tell me what God is saying to me; I just need confirmation. I do not get any words and thank God that people are afraid to even come near me with a word. You better have something that confirms, and it better not be something new because God can talk to me, and then He uses a prophet to confirm His Word. Prophets are not people who live in caves with a staff and animal skins, and they do not write the Bible anymore. The New Testament prophet does not write Scripture. The New Testament prophet confirms. We are in the age of faith now, and if you do not side with the prophecies that have been spoken over you, guess what happens? Nothing. It is by faith that you receive them. We are in the New Testament, and we walk by faith.

> *For as many as are led by the Spirit of God, these are sons of God.*
> —ROMANS 8:14

Paul did *not* say that those who are led by *prophets* are sons of God. No, he said, "Those who are *led by the Spirit* are sons of God." I have shown you a couple of ways that you can be robbed and that you do not need a middle man between you and God because you already have Jesus. Jesus is the mediator between God and man, and He is the only one. In the year 1517, Martin Luther already went through this when he nailed his 95 Theses to a church door in Germany. He started the Protestant Reformation when he stated that there was only one mediator between God and man, and that is Jesus Christ (see 1 Tim. 2:5-6). They wanted to kill Martin Luther for that.

I saw how people are being robbed in this last day, which is not the day and not the time to be deceived. I have so many friends in the last three years who are not in the ministry anymore. You do not mess up on the last lap of your race. These people have lived for God for years and years, and now they do not want to have anything to do with ministry. I am telling you that there has to be something missing if people can just leave.

It is because, *"Pure and undefiled religion before God and the Father is this: to visit orphans and widows in their trouble, and to keep oneself unspotted from the world"* (James 1:27). It is to take care of the poor, take care of people, and to watch over what you have been given. I am going to be a guardian of the assets of God. That means that you are under my care, and I will have to tell you the truth. But Paul said, *"Have I therefore become your enemy because I tell you the truth?"* (Gal. 4:16).

Peter also had unrealistic expectations. Peter spoke about the fact that Jesus was the Messiah, the Son of the living God (see Matt. 16:13-20). Jesus said to him, *"Blessed are you, Simon Bar-Jonah, for flesh and blood has not revealed this to you, but My Father who is in heaven."* Two paragraphs later, Jesus was telling His disciples that He had to go to Jerusalem and be killed and be raised on the third day (see Matt. 16:21-23).

After Jesus told His disciples everything that would happen to Him, there was no one waiting for Jesus at the tomb, even though He told them He would be raised. But Peter immediately said no, "Lord, this shall not happen to You!" Suddenly Jesus was addressing satan, and He said, looking at Peter, "Get behind me, satan!" He said, *"You are not mindful of the things of God, but the things of men"* (Matt. 16:23). Jesus knew the unrealistic expectations that they had toward Him.

Peter needed to repent, but he did not. When Peter denied the Lord three times, then he repented, and he did not even know if he was going to get back or not (see Luke 22:54-62). Peter was so surprised when Jesus came to retrieve him that he jumped out of the boat. Peter did not walk on water that day, but he did get to the shore (see John 21:7-19). Peter was surprised by Jesus' love because he thought he had blown it, but it should never have gotten to that place.

I want to get converts who become disciples. I want you to come to the Lord the right way, by discerning that God loves you and that it is His goodness that leads you to repentance. You should never feel guilty about past sin if you have repented of it. If you have asked for forgiveness, then it no longer exists. *"Repent therefore and be converted, that your sins may be blotted out, so that times of refreshing may come from the presence of the Lord"*

(Acts 3:19). This means that you should never feel guilty about your past.

> *Or do you despise the riches of His goodness, for-bearance, and longsuffering, not knowing that the goodness of God leads you to repentance?*
> —ROMANS 2:4

God is very good, and God leads His people to repentance because of His goodness. We need a dose of God's goodness.

> *But he who is spiritual judges all things, yet he him-self is rightly judged by no one. For "who has known the mind of the Lord that he may instruct Him?" But we have the mind of Christ.*
> —1 CORINTHIANS 2:15-16

What Paul is saying here is that a carnal person cannot judge a spiritual person. A spiritual man can have discernment about all things and can rightly divide with the Word of God. However, a spiritual man is not subject to any carnal man's judgment. A carnal person cannot know the things of God and cannot even accept the Spirit of God. That is why I am supposed to judge myself, so I am not subject to any man's judgment (see 1 Cor. 11:31). A spiritual person makes judgments about all things. In keeping with repentance, you will stay true, and you will not get off track.

CHECKS AND BALANCES

When I was being trained to fly, I learned certain things that I thought were very basic. I was almost rolling my eyes but then realized that they could become very handy when you were about to die. Mark Twain is credited as having said, "When I was a boy of 14, my father was so ignorant I could hardly stand to have the old man around. But when I got to be 21, I was astonished at how much the old man had learned in seven years." When it presents itself, at times wisdom is not discerned, but it is needed. As we grow older, we realize that we do not know everything we think we do, and we just want to live. After you have almost died a couple of times, you start to be more open, and repentance does that.

When I was learning to fly, they have something called "dead reckoning." With almost all airplane accidents, everything has been thoroughly analyzed afterward and recorded. You can get the cockpit recordings, all the reports, and anything that had happened in the accident. You can read through it and see all the details. I have talked to people about the black boxes as well, and I was able to ask questions about what was going on in the cockpit at the time.

There were people from the investigation board from my airline who could tell me exactly what was going on at the time of the accident. One particular plane accident I studied I knew had happened on landing. When I spoke with an investigation board member about it, he told me that the accident started over 200 miles out from the landing, and the mistakes started piling up because they were in a hurry.

When you are held accountable in the cockpit, they call it dead reckoning. The air controller would ask the pilot, "Position?" They already know your position because they have you on the radar, but you have to answer. If they ask you, "Airspeed," it is because you are speeding. If they ask, "Altitude," it is because you may have drifted down 200 feet. If you go down to 300 feet, you get a violation, and it could mean a $12,000 fine, and it is the same with speeding.

When the air controllers ask you these questions, they are giving you this one warning shot. The pilot will have to lie to the controller as they are pulling back on the throttle or yoke to readjust it. That warning shot from the controller is what I consider repentance. It is a form of checks and balances to keep you clean. You can understand why satan would want to get rid of the whole idea of repentance and try to make it something religious. Repenting once in your life does not cause you to reach perfection because it is a continual checks and balances process.

At times, the air controllers would ask the pilot questions, and the pilots would always have to know what was happening with their plane. The reason is because they could lose any one of the seven systems on the airplane, and if that happened, an annunciator panel would light up. I always thought that was just like what happens in my spirit because I can feel things inside me—red lights and green lights—and there is a warning and slow-down light too. It is the way the Spirit of God operates inside of us.

If something went wrong on a plane, the pilot would have to isolate the system that was acting up. They would go through a prepared checklist to isolate it even further and determine the problem. Many times, the problem is not sudden, and it is a series of developments. That one accident I studied started happening 220 miles out. It is the same thing with adultery and many other kinds of sin. It does not just happen. It was satan's plan, and he is trying to trip people up with anything he can.

Once the pilot starts to isolate the problem, they become very busy, but they still have to fly the airplane. If it turns quickly into something serious, you have to know your options because you cannot pull off to the side of the road in an airplane. It is the same with your life because once you are in it, you are committed, and you want to operate in your life correctly. I have found that it is best to have a repentant heart and a repentant life. I always want to refocus on Jesus and remind myself of where I am going and that I want to look the best I can for Him. It is not for myself, but it is about being excellent and being above reproach with everything as a representative of the kingdom of God.

I have to be situationally aware of my options for landing an airplane. I must know where the airports are and what the glide is because each airplane has a different glide path. If you have the engines off, you can put the airplane into a descent and keep a certain speed. Every airplane has a sweet spot, and with a 737, you can glide 60 miles and land.

The Lord taught me to be sober-minded in my Christian life and not let things continue to develop in a contrary way. If God is trying to tell you, "Hey, this is not right," it gives you time to back out. It gives you time to have more options. You do not want to get into a situation where satan has you to the point where you are trapped. Religion will do that, religion will get you into traps, and it is hard to back out of things.

THE THOUGHTS OF GOD

You need to start discerning and know that something is not right here or something is good here. You must discern the way you are going to walk in it, and that is how you start to develop your spiritual discernment and sensitivity to the Holy Spirit. You become tuned into what God is doing, and then we are all tuned in together as the body because we are all part of the body of Christ.

> *But as it is written: "Eye has not seen, nor ear heard, Nor have entered into the heart of man the things which God has prepared for those who love Him." But God has revealed them to us through His Spirit. For the Spirit searches all things, yes, the deep things of God. For what man knows the things of a man except the spirit of the man which is in him? Even so no one knows the things of God except the Spirit of God.*
> —1 CORINTHIANS 2:9-11

Think of the Spirit of God as being in the Father. The Spirit knows the thoughts of the Father, but our spirit knows our thoughts. So if you put the Spirit of God in your spirit, then you can know the thoughts of God. That is what is being said here. The Holy Spirit has told me that many people have been through so much trouble and trauma, and they are tired of being wrong all the time. They do not want to be wrong, but I am finding that it is better to ask for help than to die.

In my time being a pilot, there were times when I had to ask for help, but I had to come to a decision. If I do not ask for help, I will die because I cannot figure out what is going on here, and I only have a certain amount of time to figure it out. You would not believe the stuff that I have been through, and my instructor had to call me every day and make me go back to the airplane because I had so many things happen that you could get traumatized. My instructor would call me and say, "Meet me at the airplane." I told him, "You know, I do not want to be a pilot anymore. I just want to live."

What the instructor knew was that I had to get back in the saddle. I had to learn to make that airplane do what I wanted it to do instead of taking me places that I did not want to go. I found out that I was not aggressive enough in the right things and that it is good to be aggressive in the right things. Just like you have to be fully convinced of the Word of God.

You have to be fully convinced of what God is saying to you. The spirit realm is so convincing to me now, but it never used to be that way because I did not know the spiritual realm. The reason is that I would not admit its reality because I was prideful. When I died and went to Heaven and I came back, I lost all my pride because I realized that I could do nothing without Jesus. However, I could have read that instead of dying to find it out. *I am the vine, you are the branches. He who abides in Me, and I in him, bears much fruit; for without Me you can do nothing"* (John 15:5). I saw that I was following people who were very prideful in the ministry.

There is a boldness and confidence that we can have without being prideful. The best pilots were the kindest, nicest people, but they knew their stuff. I would watch how they would handle the airplane, and I learned so much from them. I would ask them, "Why do you do that? Why do you do this?" They would have eight scars to show why they do it that way now.

I have spiritual parents above me, and I always put myself under those who are smarter than me, who have been doing what they do for many more years than I probably ever will. Everyone I hire is better at what they do than me, and that is why I hired them. I do not want people to make me feel bad because I do not know everything. After all, that is not why I hired them. I hired them to help me and cause what we are doing to expand outward, and even though it takes more people than me, that is okay.

I found out that my spiritual fathers do things a certain way because they have already experienced it. Through the anointing, God has been able to implement the boundaries because they are very humble people. I saw the humility in people above me asking for help from me, and it melts you like butter. Everyone who got somewhere got there because someone else helped them. They had wisdom, but someone else paved the way. We are not in this just by ourselves, and unrealistic expectations can rob you of God's agenda and cause you to be in pride.

You might not know you missed God until you hit a wall. Many people have not judged themselves, and because of that they are fading away, but they should not be. I have watched satan come in, and I believe it is because we do not keep turning our focus back to where we are going, which is Jesus. Ask Jesus to reveal to you your true condition.

As you saw in the Laodicean church, Jesus' revelation was completely opposite to what they thought of themselves. Notice that none of the seven churches listed in Revelation exist anymore in Turkey. Half of them became mosques, and the others are just gone. Jesus tried to warn them. Two thousand years have passed since these people lived, but I do not want to find myself in that spot.

YOU CANNOT SERVE GOD AND MAMMON

The best advice that I can give you that I got from Heaven is to stay humble and remember that your life is a gift. For you to be effective in this life, it is more about yielding to Jesus and letting Him blow into your life and give you life than to think that you have the ability to do these things on your own.

Why is it that in the New Testament, Jesus said it is hard for a rich man to get to Heaven? (see Matt. 19:24-26). Paul said that the love of money, *not money*, is a root of all kinds of evil (see 1 Tim. 6:10). Jesus said that you cannot serve God and mammon (see Matt. 6:24). When I was in Heaven, I saw that the kingdom of God was God's way of doing things and that He had a kingdom. There was the kingdom of Heaven, which is up there and beautiful, and then there is the kingdom of God moving on the earth through men and advancing.

On earth, you have the manifestation of the move of God where the Gospel is preached, and when the people hear the message and turn, then they are saved. It is important to realize that people do not get raptured as soon as they get saved, and they are still here. It is not good enough to just pluck people out of hell because they still have to live here. I was sent back from Heaven to help people live down here successfully in the power of God.

When I came back, everyone was buying DVDs on the end times, and they were buying food and storing food and waiting for all this stuff to happen. I saw that Paul wrote two letters to the Thessalonians and said, *"If anyone will not work, neither shall he eat"* (2 Thess. 3:10). Paul said that the coming of the Lord would not happen until he who is holding him back is removed (see 2 Thess. 2:6-8). The Lord showed me that who is holding the lawless one back is the church. It is the Holy Spirit. The Thessalonians were thinking that Jesus was coming back right away, so they were quitting their jobs. Every generation seems to go through this.

When I was in Heaven, I saw that God was not against people being rich. God was against people being greedy, selfish, and hoarding riches to where they needed to repent. They had allowed riches to grab them and grab their attention, and it pulled them away from God. I saw that God does not want to lose people. Jesus told me, "If I give My people everything they are asking for, they will go to the lake in that new boat instead of going to church. And they will have a tailgate party with that brand-new truck at the football game." Jesus said, "I am not against people being rich, but it is hard for a rich man to get to Heaven because it draws you away."

In the parable of the soils, Jesus talked about one of the things that caused the thorns to choke out the Word of God and cause it to become unfruitful (see Mark 4:18-19). Jesus said it was the cares of this life and the deceitfulness of riches. Jesus said these things because it is not the money that is evil; it is the love of money. Anything that takes your attention away from God is wrong.

> But seek first the kingdom of God and His righteousness, and all these things shall be added to you.
> —MATTHEW 6:33

Jesus instructed me, and He said, "If you can master and be the master of your domain and rule and reign, you can have all of these things if you seek first the kingdom." If you seek the *things*, they will always evade you. You will always be pursuing them, and you are never going to have enough. You will always want the newest model, you will always want another raise, and you will always need more. This world is set up in a poverty mentality and a debt mentality so that you never really achieve everything that you want to by participating in the world's system. Repentance keeps you true so that you keep your focus. Then what will happen is wealth will begin to pursue *you*.

God is not withholding anything from you. God says, *"No good thing will He withhold from those who walk uprightly"* (Ps. 84:11). I found that this is what it is; it is repentance. Our enemy, satan, got the church to misrepresent what repentance really means. Then because it does not fit the definition given of it in Scripture, it does not fit the culture anymore. It then becomes easy for them to pull it out and say it has become offensive.

The Gospel is confronting, but the enemy has come in with tares and sown among the wheat, and the goats are among the sheep. Jesus was constantly combating the religious system, but He was giving grace to the humble. Jesus was not resisting the humble; He was resisting the proud, and He pushed them back (see James 4:6).

When I was in Heaven, I saw that when God trusts you, He starts asking you what *you* want. That might sound so foreign to you right now, but I have had the Lord ask me what I want because, He said, "I trust you." I said, "What?" I was more than surprised. How did this come to pass? It was because I saw that my life is not my own anymore (see Gal. 2:20). I now live by faith in the Son of God and He lives and moves and has His being in me, and I can flow in Him (see Acts 17:28).

I was speaking at MorningStar Ministries, and I started talking just like I usually do. Suddenly I said, "There is a witch in here, and I am giving you two minutes to repent, or you are going to hell." Then I said, "I am going to cast those devils out, and their familiar spirits will no longer be able to operate through you. You are going to lose your power, and you and those devils are going to go through that door. You have two minutes." And I stood there and waited for two minutes. I felt like I had a staff in my hand.

A woman came up to repent, and devil voices started screaming out of her. I noticed that she had a book from my book table called, *Why Speak in Tongues?* As I lay hands on her, the devils came out, and then she started speaking in tongues. I want to tell you that the other environment, the heavenly kingdom, the one you seek, that kingdom goes with you and assists you.

As you pursue God in that realm, what happens is all these other things are added to you. When the people witnessed that woman's deliverance, many others started coming up to repent. I just kept asking, "Okay, what do you want to repent of?" Each one said, "I want to repent of this or that," and did so. Someone said after that, if I had given an altar call right there, half the room would have come up. I realized that if repentance is so bad, why does everyone want to do it?

I got a dose from the other realm when I was in Heaven, and I saw that God is not withholding things from us. God wants us to come into alignment in our spirit with Him and be settled that He is a good Father. The Lord has asked me to ask you, "What is inside of you that God has placed there, that satan has done everything he can to keep you from exploding and from allowing it to come out?"

You will succeed in the mission that God has placed within you. That is a prophecy that you can take and wage war with because I was in your future, and I saw the end. Everyone who had repented and walked with God was saved, and we were all worshiping in Heaven at God's throne and so thankful. Now take that future and walk it back to where you are right now. I was in the future and was sent back, and now I am just acting it out. It is a play, and I know the scene, and I know what to say because it is already written in Heaven.

I am showing you that your opportunity is right before you. You must find out what is inside of you because the limitations are being taken off your life, and you must meet the needs of the people. From now on, when you think of repentance, think of a long-range rifle with a scope on it. You do not treat it like a pistol; you use the scope because it is a precision instrument, and repentance causes you to be precise. It is important for you to produce fruit in keeping with repentance (see Matt. 3:8-10).

ASK, SEEK, AND KNOCK

Ask, and it will be given to you; seek, and you will find; knock, and it will be opened to you. For everyone who asks receives, and he who seeks finds, and to him who knocks it will be opened. Or what man is there among you who, if his son asks for bread, will give him a stone? Or if he asks for a fish, will he give him a serpent? If you then, being evil, know how to give good gifts to your children, how much more will your Father who is in heaven give good things to those who ask Him!

—MATTHEW 7:7-11

I saw in Heaven that there are people who are resistant to the concept expressed in this verse. However, you *can* actually ask and receive, seek and find, and knock, and the door shall be open to you by your heavenly Father. Period. What is God saying, what is He doing? *Everyone* who asks receives, and he who seeks finds, and to him who knocks, it will be opened.

If you think that this is way too much already, then he goes even further. He starts to explain that there is a loving, kind heavenly Father who reveals His goodness to us, and it leads us to repentance.

I am the vine, you are the branches. He who abides in Me, and I in him, bears much fruit; for without Me you can do nothing. If anyone does not abide in Me, he is cast out as a branch and is withered; and they gather them and throw them into the fire, and they are burned. If you abide in Me, and My words abide in you, you will ask what you desire, and it shall be done for you.

—JOHN 15:5-7

I saw that when you are walking with God in repentance, there is fruit that is produced. The fruit is that *"you will ask what you desire, and it shall be done for you."* When you are abiding in the vine, and Jesus is abiding in you, you can ask what you will. Whatever you desire will be given to you. Repentance is so profound, and I found that it is what needs to happen in the body of Christ, and the quicker the better. We have to provoke the Jews to jealousy, and the last time I checked they are doing better than we are in a lot of areas.

For, there is one God and one Mediator who can reconcile God and humanity—the man Christ Jesus. He gave his life to purchase freedom for everyone. This is the message God gave to the world at just the right time.

—1 TIMOTHY 2:5-6 NLT

I will keep my focus on Him just like you do, and we are going to finish above and beyond, with excellence. We are going to provoke people to jealousy, and they are going to want to be

Christians. Do not just present people with fire insurance, but let them know the love of God, which leads to repentance. It makes it a lot easier when people come to the Lord for the right reason. They need a revelation of the Father and His goodness.

We are not getting the things we ask because we ask amiss to spend it on our pleasures (see James 4:3). We do not understand the ways of the Father. If we knew God and His character, we would know that He would not deny us because we would not ask amiss. We are not going to ask according to our own selfish desires.

Someone called me whom I have never met and said, "The Lord just told me I am supposed to give you this. Is this true?" I said, "Yes." And there have been things that have come to me that I told the Lord about personally when He asked me a question. I am never going to ask anyone for these things because they come from God. You would not believe how many times these sorts of things have happened.

I have learned that God is my Father, and my trust in Him can cause things to go the way they are supposed to go. I agree with God's revealed will for me, but that is through the Holy Spirit and the Word of God. I do not have to tell people what I am believing for because it is not through manipulation.

Not that I have already attained, or am already perfected; but I press on, that I may lay hold of that for which Christ Jesus has also laid hold of me. Brethren, I do not count myself to have apprehended; but one thing I do, forgetting those things

*which are behind and reaching forward to those
things which are ahead, I press toward the goal for
the prize of the upward call of God in Christ Jesus.*
—Philippians 3:12-14

Understand that the demons cannot do much about someone who has decided that they are not going to be knocked out of
the race and that they are going to keep their focus on Jesus. You
need to stay in the love of God, and that is where God's power is.
You build yourself up in your most holy of faith, praying in the
Holy Spirit, and keeping in the love of God (see Jude 1:20-21).
The Spirit of God will keep you there because there is no fear in
love; perfect love casts out fear because fear involves torment. He
who fears has not been made perfect in love (see 1 John 4:18-20).

*Therefore, brethren, be even more diligent to make
your call and election sure, for if you do these things
you will never stumble; for so an entrance will be
supplied to you abundantly into the everlasting
kingdom of our Lord and Savior Jesus Christ.*
—2 Peter 1:10-11

If you do these things, you will never stumble. An entrance
will be supplied to you so abundantly into the everlasting kingdom of our Lord Jesus Christ.

Chapter 4

Do Not Be an Unbelieving Believer

Jesus said to him, "If you can believe, all things are possible to him who believes." Immediately the father of the child cried out and said with tears, "Lord, I believe; help my unbelief!"

—MARK 9:23-24

THERE IS THIS new hybrid believer, and it is called an unbelieving believer, and they have infiltrated the body of Christ. They are unbelieving believers. It is an oxymoron. In this verse in Mark, the father was humble enough when he said to Jesus, "I do believe; help my unbelief!" He turned himself in. Did you know that faith is of the heart? Jesus said that when you believe in your heart that what you say with your mouth shall come to pass, you shall have it (see Rom. 10:9). It does not say if you believe in your head, but it is *believe in your heart*. Faith is of the heart, and it is a gift of God. There is a problem with an unbelieving believer because faith is of the heart, and you can have doubt in your mind but believe in your heart. It is satan who comes into your mind, and that is why you must bring into captivity every thought to the obedience of Christ (see 2 Cor. 10:5). You want to get your mind to side with the truth, and this is spiritual warfare.

We hear so many people talking about their faith. In First Corinthians 13:13 (NIV), we read, *"And now these three remain: faith, hope and love. But the greatest of these is faith."* NO! It is *love*, *"the greatest of these is love."* Yet we hear faith, faith, faith all the time. I would rather fall on the mercy of God and say, "God, You love me, and I need to learn how to love You. I need to learn how to love myself. I need to let You love on me, and I need Your help."

It is amazing how that father turned himself in, and Jesus gave him what he asked for when he said, "I do believe, help my unbelief." What was happening with that father was that faith is of the heart, but he wanted a deeper relationship with Jesus just like we do. But we do not always have the capability of operating in that realm. Once you turn and you face God, you will face Jesus; you will look into His eyes, you have a relationship with Him, and you know He wants to give you what you desire. I saw it in His eyes. Can He trust you?

WHAT HE SAYS IS WHO HE IS

When I was in Heaven, Jesus showed me what faith was to me. There was a stack of papers on the desk, and Jesus knew I wanted to ask Him what they were. Jesus said, "Those are all the prayer requests you are ever going to ask." He said, "They are already signed by you and Me." All of a sudden, I trusted in the power of God, not just what He says, but on who God is because they are the same. Whatever God says, there is no difference between what He says and who He is. There is no discrepancy. However, down here, what people say and what they do are two different things.

I realized that the Lord is not playing a game with us. If I told you the full force of what Jesus did for us, it would usher in the end times. We need to engage God in a relationship that we cannot fail and that the limits are taken off. I do not want to make you feel good about where you are because that is not how the kingdom works. I was sent back for a reason, and that is to be like a plumb line, a measuring rod to a generation (see Amos 7:7-8). People are going to knock against a plumb line because everything is fine until the plumb line shows up. Everything crooked is called straight until the plumb line comes.

Isaiah was a major prophet, and everything was fine with him until Isaiah 6. Suddenly, Isaiah found himself in the throne room of God. *"Woe is me, for I am undone! Because I am a man of unclean lips"* (Isa. 6:5). He was fine a minute before. That is why we need a move of God, why we need the Word of God preached, and why we need the Spirit of God to come in at a higher level.

We need to have to crawl to our cars afterward. We need to be introduced to more.

I was introduced to more, and I did not think I was coming back. I saw that all my prayer requests were already stacked and listed and that it was the title deed. *"Faith is the substance of things hoped for, the evidence of things not seen"* (Heb. 11:1). I had the title deed of what I had believed for, and faith was the substance for what I hoped for, and I had the evidence. My trust is based on my revelation of who God is, not just what He says. He is a good God, and He can perform what He says.

You can quote the Word of God over and over again, but I am not going to convince God if I say it 500 times. God is not going to say, "You know what? Please go down there and give him this because I am tired of hearing it." I do not have to wear my Father out. Jesus only marveled at two people's faith in Scripture, and they were not Israelites.

The two people with the most exceptional faith were the centurion and the Samaritan woman. The centurion said to Jesus, "Lord, I am not worthy for You to come to my house. Only speak a word, and my servant will be healed" (see Matt. 8:5-13). The centurion explained that he was a man under authority and understood authority. Jesus marveled when He heard that and said, "I have not found such great faith, not even in Israel."

In Heaven, I saw that faith has more to do with authority and getting under authority. You must let it settle into your heart that the limitations have been taken off because God is speaking for you. It is not just saying things. It is because of who God is. Did you know that when God says something, there are countless levels of revelation in His intent for why He said what He said? It is not only about the words God uses, but it is also about God's intent.

When I was in Heaven, the Holy Spirit gave me seven different interpretations and levels of the Old Testament Scriptures for everything God spoke to me. The Holy Spirit was behind me, saying, "This is in Deuteronomy, and this is what Moses said, and this has to do with that." I saw that the whole revelation of God in the Bible fits intricately together, and it is all revelation. What Jesus was saying were types and shadows that were in the Old Testament.

I know that Jesus is not the problem with anything that is *not* happening in our life. I saw that God could never be accused of anything, so I am pushing the responsibility back onto you. If you stood before Jesus and you got to see Him as He is, and you realized that Jesus has never been wrong, then you are never going to tell Him that it was His fault for anything that happened to you. I saw that I am never going to tell Jesus that His blood was not enough, that His name was not enough for the demons to leave, and that the stripes on His back were not enough to heal cancer. I saw that Jesus is exceedingly above all that we could ask or think, according to the power that works in us (see Eph. 3:20). So if we are in lack, it is not His fault.

Can you try to go in your spirit right now and think about what it would be like to stand before the Head of the church, Jesus Christ, who said, *"If you can believe, all things are possible to him who believes"* (Mark 9:23)? What do you say after that? Are you going to tell Jesus that you are the exception to the rule? Be honest right now. Immediately, that father of the sick child cried out, *"Lord, I believe; help my unbelief."* That is what you need to do. How many times did Jesus say, "Why did you doubt? It was because of your unbelief"?

THE LEAST IN THE KINGDOM IS GREATER

While it is said: "Today, if you will hear His voice, do not harden your hearts as in the rebellion." For who, having heard, rebelled? Indeed, was it not all who came out of Egypt, led by Moses? Now with whom was He angry forty years? Was it not with those who sinned, whose corpses fell in the wilderness? And to whom did He swear that they would not enter His rest, but to those who did not obey? So we see that they could not enter in because of unbelief.
— HEBREWS 3:15-19

It says here that the Israelites fell in the desert because of their unbelief. Because of their unbelief, they did not enter into the Promised Land. This Scripture then warns us not to be like them, and the writer is talking to *believers*. Accountability comes in right here. This is for believers who want to walk in the power of God and want to see miracles and want angels to be standing at their bedside. If you want that, know that it is not only for the apostles and the prophets. It is for anyone who comes after John the Baptist. Jesus said, *"Assuredly, I say to you, among those born of women there has not risen one greater than John the Baptist; but he who is least in the kingdom of heaven is greater than he"* (Matt.

11:11). The least in the kingdom is greater than John, *and that is us* and all who believe from now on!

You need to turn yourself in. You do not see the results you want because you have not turned yourself in, and you are trying to make your faith work. First of all, you do not *try* anything. God has never tried a thing because He has already determined in His heart what He wants, and then God does it. God made us in His image, but we live in a broken world, and it is fallen and does not function well. We get frustrated because we are Spirit-filled and born again, and we operate on a higher level, but we are in a fallen world. We cannot always understand why things are not working quickly enough because we know God is a good God.

When push comes to shove, it is only a spiritual response that satan understands. When you decide that you will not move off what God has already said, the war begins. *"Therefore take up the whole armor of God, that you may be able to withstand in the evil day, and having done all, to stand"* (Eph. 6:13). This Scripture does not even say that you have to use that armor. Have it on, but when you have done all, stand.

I saw in Heaven that a believer on the earth is someone to be feared by the enemy. My wife and I see this all the time when we go to prayer. We think it will take five or six hours in prayer, and in ten minutes we are through and start laughing. We would see white flags being put up, and the enemy was surrendering, and it was a quick thing. I am telling you now that you need to turn yourself in because things are not happening if you do not realize that you are in a war.

You are very complicated; just ask your friends. God has intricately made you, and man was not created to be in a fallen world. We were never meant to die. Once you get to Heaven, you will not think about it anymore because you will know it. You can know it now if you see what Jesus Christ did and how He bought us back so that we can be believing ones and have signs following us. It was for the Father's purpose to bring in the harvest.

Did you know that healing is not just for us? Healing is for the unsaved to bring them into the kingdom. We are supposed to be walking in *divine health*. Why did the Old Testament children of Israel never get sick in the desert? God said, *"I will take sickness away from the midst of you"* (Exod. 23:25). Why didn't their shoes ever wear out? Why did their clothes never wear out? How do you provide water and food for two and a half million people in the desert? That was the Old Testament, and now our promises in the New Testament are based on even greater promises.

I saw that the power that raised Jesus from the dead, the Holy Spirit, lives in us and will also give *life* to our mortal bodies (see Rom. 8:11). I also saw there was a transference of the power of God that could come into your flesh if by the Spirit you put to death the misdeeds of the body, which could be a disease, and you will live (see Rom. 8:13). Anything that exalts itself above the knowledge of God must be brought into captivity (see 2 Cor. 10:5).

If you look online at the latest microscopes, you can see that when they enlarge the size of bacteria and parasites, they look like something out of Jurassic Park. They look like mini dinosaurs, and they are ugly creatures, and they are in your body. They are also intelligent because they know how to morph and to resist. They know how to weaken your immune system so that they cannot be fought back anymore. Now that is demonic.

I have never fasted or prayed for any of the heavenly encounters that I have had. I have never asked Jesus to appear to me, and I have never asked the angels to come to me. I would never pray for it now because I have had so many things happen that I cannot handle it. I know how holy God's angels are. I have the fear of the Lord, knowing what it is like to be on the floor shaking and asking God to please leave so that I do not die. I felt like my flesh was going to fall off my bones.

I asked the Lord, "Lord, how much can I take and still stay alive?" That is what I want. What can I take and still be able to walk away? And I am finding out. What I experienced on the other side is what we are supposed to be experiencing down here now. No one wants to be brave enough to say it because it seems unattainable by way of our life down here. However, these heavenly experiences, because they are so strong, sometimes I do not know if I can function, and it is very hard on my body.

I have asked God to show me certain things. I have asked about altar fire, holiness, giving, receiving, repentance, and waiting on God. All these different words—the crucified life, the blood of Jesus, all of these very powerful words—they seem to have been taken out of our vocabulary.

When I asked the Lord to show me what holiness is, sometimes I wish I had never asked. I was an unbelieving believer concerning holiness, but I did not know it. You can think that holiness does not mean what it used to mean anymore, or that God understands, and He loves you just the way you are.

THE POWERS OF THE COMING AGE

Something happened in Seattle, and my wife Kathi remembers the day it happened because of how it came to me, and I still have not gotten over it. When I asked God to help me understand those things taken from our vocabulary, I was on an airplane to Seattle with my wife. I specifically asked God what the powers of the coming age were that were mentioned in Hebrews 6. There are those who have tasted the heavenly gift and have become partakers of the Holy Spirit and have tasted the powers of the coming age. If they then trample underfoot the blood of Jesus as though it is nothing, then there is no repentance for that sin. I had never focused on the fact that there was no repentance, as in "the unpardonable sin."

I only wanted to know if I should have already tasted of the powers of the coming age. I wanted to know that if I had already encountered it, why wasn't it forefront in my mind and maybe I had to go into it deeper. A part of my mind was unbelieving because I did not believe in certain things until they started happening.

While I was on the airplane to Seattle sitting next to my wife, I asked God about all of these things. Suddenly an angel came and took me. I cannot explain it, but I looked and saw my wife still sitting there as I left the airplane. The angel took me back to Enoch's time, and I saw Enoch walking in a forested area. He was just coming up to a clearing where there was an open field. I could see the power of God that was all around him.

The angel said, "The Lord has sent me to show you and explain to you the powers of the coming age." He said, "Behold, the powers of the coming age!" When he said that, I looked, and Enoch, who was on his left foot, was putting his right foot in front of him to step, and it disappeared. The power of God came around him, and the Spirit of God wrapped him up and took him up in his body. The angel said, "Behold the powers of the coming age."

Then the angel grabbed me again, and he took me on the other side of the flood to Elijah, and I saw Elijah get taken up. Again I saw the power of God, and like a blanket the Holy Spirit wrapped around him and took Elijah's body up with a whirlwind and fire. The angel again said, "Behold the powers of the coming age!" Right then, I realized that I do not know a thing because these two men of God are in Heaven right now with their bodies.

Moses spent time with God. All of the Israelites were supposed to be up on Mount Sinai to meet with God, but only Moses went up. Moses spent two 40-day periods with God that we know of, as written in Exodus 24 and Exodus 34. Moses had a Psalm 91 experience there with God. When Moses came down the second time, the people could not stand to look at him because Moses' face radiated light, and they asked him to wear a veil over his face because they were afraid.

Jesus told me that He was there on Mount Sinai with Moses and that Moses spoke face to face with Him. Jesus told me that what the disciples saw on the Mount of Transfiguration was

Jesus and Moses when they talked on Mount Sinai (see Matt. 17:2-8). Elijah was translated back to Mount Sinai, and they were all meeting on Mount Sinai.

On the Mount of Transfiguration, after seeing Moses and Elijah, Peter wanted them to build three tabernacles to commemorate it, but Jesus must have been rolling His eyes. He could see that Peter was not getting it. Jesus was trying to show the disciples, "This is who I was before you were born." Peter, James, and John got to see Jesus being transfigured, but Jesus was showing them that He was pre-existent. Elijah was just walking one day and got translated back to Mount Sinai. Moses was just talking to Jesus on the Mount, receiving the law. Wherever Jesus is, is the center of everything. I saw all this, and then the angel handed me a scroll, and he said, "Here is your ministry."

My ministry was to be the whole fifth chapter of Second Corinthians. I did not know what it said at the time, but this chapter, written by Paul the apostle, is focused on the Ministry of Reconciliation. We are to go out as ambassadors of Christ and tell people that the price has been paid, imploring people to be reconciled to God and accept the gift of salvation that has been given to them through Jesus' work on the cross. They can accept this gift by repenting and giving their life to Jesus Christ as Lord. Then they become a new creature, and the old things pass away, and everything becomes new. The angel said, "This is the power of the coming age." Then he said, "Kevin, you go, and you raise people from the dead spiritually, not just physically."

SEEING THE INVISIBLE

When I went to Heaven and came back, Jesus told me that I could not lose, and it is all extra credit. That is how it is in Heaven, and we are to pray that the kingdom would come on this earth as it is in Heaven. That God's will be done on the earth as it is in Heaven. Well, how is it in Heaven? We are supposed to be seated with Him and then bring it back here and implement it into an imperfect world, and we are not supposed to doubt. We are supposed to believe, and the reason is that our belief is sight, our spiritual sight.

Your spiritual eyes are seeing the things that are invisible. The Scripture says that the people of faith saw Him who was invisible (see Heb. 11:27). They were looking for a city whose builder and maker was God (see Heb. 11:10). They saw Him who was invisible, so understand that faith is not something that you conjure up. It is a seed that you plant. It has to be a small seed, like a mustard seed, but it produces a crop if you plant it. So it is a mystery. You have the substance if you have a seed.

> *Whoever eats My flesh and drinks My blood has eternal life, and I will raise him up at the last day. For My flesh is food indeed, and My blood is drink indeed. He who eats My flesh and drinks My blood abides in Me, and I in him.*
> —JOHN 6:54-56

Here are some of the key entrances to getting rid of your unbelief. Jesus said, *"Whoever eats My flesh and drinks My blood has eternal life."* From that time, many of Jesus' disciples who heard him that day left Him and followed Him no more (see John 6:66). Jesus was saying that they were following Him because they were being fed and were seeing miracles. They were spectators, but they did not know God's ways.

God, through Jesus Christ, is giving them the way, but He whittled it down to a small Bible study where before Jesus had a mega-church following Him. *"For My flesh is food indeed.... He who eats My flesh and drinks My blood abides in Me, and I in him."* The people did not spiritually grasp what Jesus was saying because they were mentally involved with Him, which is how Christianity is today.

If you do not like something today, you quit giving to people, and you walk away even if it is the truth. You say, "I am not giving to them anymore," or "I am not going to come to their meetings anymore." If you want the truth, the truth will set you free (see John 8:31). However, if you do not hear the truth, you will be entrapped. When Jesus came and spoke the truth, He was correcting, because He wanted them to be free.

Jesus said, *"I am the living bread which came down from Heaven"* (John 6:51). That is the representation of His body and His blood. The life of the flesh is in the blood (see Lev. 17:11), and when you accept Jesus, sin is gone because the atonement is in the blood. Jesus' blood was perfect in His generations, and He was a spotless Lamb.

Jesus' sacrifice was enough, and this is the entrance into belief from unbelief. You become part of Him. Jesus is the vine, and you are the branches. The life comes through the vine into you, and after that, *"You can ask what you will, and it shall be done for you"* (John 15:7). All because life is in the vine, and you are part of that. You never want to become disconnected from the vine because that is what connects you to life in Jesus.

> *If the world hates you, you know that it hated Me*
> *before it hated you. If you were of the world, the*
> *world would love its own. Yet because you are not of*
> *the world, but I chose you out of the world, therefore*
> *the world hates you.*
>
> —JOHN 15:18-19

You must accept that you are just visiting here, and this is not your home. You are not to spend your energy trying to fit in. I had only been in the ministry for two years when the Lord said to me, "I never called you to convert goats to sheep." So, I never argue with anyone about anything. I have not been sent back to defend myself or what happened to me. I am sent back to tell who Jesus is, what it is like in Heaven, and how we can walk in the kingdom down here on earth. Jesus told me to come back and tell people what I saw and what I heard and not defend my position. When you approach a goat, he has already locked his legs, and whatever you do, he will do the opposite.

What I saw was that if the demonic were taken away, no believer would ever doubt or fear again. I saw that as a born-again Christian, it is impossible for you to be anything other than like your Father. As a Christian in an imperfect world, I saw that you could be tossed and tempted from the outside. You can be influenced demonically from the outside, but not from the inside, because the demons do not have access to your spirit. However, they can speak to your mind, but they cannot read your thoughts. That is why they suggest things to you and then observe you to see your reaction.

Familiar spirits are assigned to you, and they keep notes. These spirits say things and do things to you. If in any way you are bothered or affected by what is being said or done by them, they begin a cycle of rejection against you. If you do not respond, they go on to something else. If you never respond, they leave you alone. If you think you are missing out on something by following God, you do not know how good your Father is, and that is an entrance for an evil spirit.

The serpent was very cunning in the garden, and he asked Eve, *"Has God indeed said…?"* He went on to tell her, *"You will not surely die. For God knows that in the day you eat of it your eyes will be opened, and you will be like God, knowing good and evil"* (Gen. 3:1-5). Genesis 1:26 says they were already like God because they were made in the image of God. Evil spirits are enforcing a curse that was placed on the earth by God. However, the curse was a result of disobedience. It happened because of our disobedience, but the demons enforce the curse while angels of God enforce the blessing.

When you choose not to respond to the demonic, they will leave you for someone weaker. The idea is not to respond. As Paul said, *"But put on the Lord Jesus Christ, and make no provision for the flesh, to fulfill its lusts"* (Rom. 13:14). Paul was saying that because demons are watching you to see how you respond to suggestions. So your unbelief is really not yours, but if you take it in and you have issues, then it disables you from being all that you are supposed to be. It might take you a while to process all this, but we do not have much time left, and Jesus told me that. I know how to defeat the devil because Jesus taught us how to do it.

You Cannot Fail

Ho! Everyone who thirsts, come to the waters; and you who have no money, come, buy and eat. Yes, come, buy wine and milk without money and without price. Why do you spend money for what is not bread, and your wages for what does not satisfy? Listen carefully to Me, and eat what is good, and let your soul delight itself in abundance. Incline your ear, and come to Me. Hear, and your soul shall live; and I will make an everlasting covenant with you—the sure mercies of David.
—Isaiah 55:1-3

You need to go over this verse every day because it will keep you corrected from getting into unbelief about what God is offering to you. Many Christians do not approach God correctly because they are unsure whether He wants to do what they need or want. They are not sure where God stands on a lot of things. I am almost 60 years old, and I am finding the things I should have known when I was 19 when I got saved. I am still doing okay, and so are you, but there is an acceleration now in these days. I am starting to see that I need to come in out of the rain. I wondered why I was getting wet, and it is obvious to me that these Scriptures, even though they are Old Testament, saw into the New Testament. None of the prophets were Old Testament because they were speaking from the future, and that is what the prophetic is.

It was because of this verse in Isaiah that I wanted to be more like Jesus, and I wanted you to get into the frame of mind of how the kingdom of God works. You can sit at the feet of Jesus and listen to Him teach, and it is through the ministry gifts of other people. However, you must discern who is speaking from that realm, and they are the ones you must choose to sit under then. I can hear Jesus' voice in certain people, but you must be discerning.

Again, this verse in Isaiah greatly influenced me because I saw that God did not want me to spend my money on that which was not bread or use my wages for that which does not satisfy. There is an exchange that happens where you come and buy without money and offer yourself up. You give yourself to God, and God exchanges with you something from the other realm, and you get an impartation. I sometimes have more questions than I have answers because I do not always understand God's favor.

God has told some people to pay our house off, and then they paid two houses off. These are huge things that have happened, and either you believe in what I am teaching you or you would get mad because it is not fair. Favor is not fair. Jesus told me if I go back, "You cannot fail." Jesus said, "With Me, you can do all things (see Phil. 4:13). *"Without Me you can do nothing"* (John 15:5). Jesus said, *"If you can believe, all things are possible to him who believes"* (Mark 9:23). I have not had anyone on this earth talk to me the way Jesus did, in the language with which He spoke to me.

If what has happened to me had happened to you, then you would want to tell everyone about Jesus. You would always want to represent Him correctly and always accommodate the manifestation of the Gospel in your life. You would not want a discrepancy between what you are experiencing and what is being said. I would be depriving you of the truth if I compromised and did not tell you the truth.

Jesus was only three feet away when He said, "If you go back, you cannot fail." He said, "You have already accomplished everything." To that, I said, "I am 31 years old. How could I have accomplished everything?" Jesus said, "It does not matter. The quality of your life is what counts, not the quantity. You have done everything that I have ever asked you to do." Then He said, "However, if you would like to go back, I will give you extra credit. It will be all extra credit, and you cannot fail. You will not lose."

When I came back, it took three weeks for the anesthesia to wear off. I was sick. All my organs hurt from what I went through. I was in Heaven for a week, but I was only gone 45 minutes, and the doctors could not determine that I was even dead. I was having a routine surgical removal of an impacted wisdom tooth. In those days, they did not monitor your heart when they did those kinds of surgeries. Now they do because of things that happened like with me, and others who have claimed that they had died and come back. I told the doctors everything that happened in the room during the operation. How could I have known that information if I was out?

When I came back, within weeks things started happening to me. I had a singing engagement and was supposed to be singing with a guy named Israel Houghton. He worked at a church but did not earn enough money to support himself, and I helped him financially by working extra with him because I believed in him. I was trained professionally to sing, but I could not play any instruments. When I came back from Heaven, I started to realize months later that I could play instruments.

Now, I had just come back from the dead a couple of weeks, and Jesus showed up. He said, "You are not singing with Israel and Kim Clement this weekend. You are going to Seattle because you are going to meet your wife." My wife was waiting for me in Seattle, but I had not met her yet! I got on a plane and went to Seattle, and I met Kathi. The Lord had told me what church to go to and that He picked her out. So I went and grabbed her and brought her back. It was not quite that easy; it actually took four months before we were married.

Miracle after miracle started happening. It was beyond what we could imagine when someone came and paid off our house. Then the Lord told us to buy another house as an investment, and someone paid that house off. The Lord kept doing what He said He would do. Jesus had rigged it all in my favor so that everything was already provided for me if I came back. So it did not surprise me when the next thing that happened was someone left us $1.4 million.

Try to imagine that I am just like you, and I am having everything that you could ever dream of wanting to happen, and it has happened. I wanted to be a pilot, but I could not afford the $250,000 for training. God told a Mormon to give me all my training for free. As soon as that happened, more things started happening.

Kathi and I were late to church because we had forgotten about the time change. As we walked in a little late and sat down, a prophet who was there said, "You two get up here. The Lord wants me to talk to you about the next million that is coming." Now, no one in the church knew about the first million because they would all want it, so we had never told anyone.

We still drove what we called the "kittie car." This car was so little that only cats could fit into it. We always felt that the money we had was God's money, and we started portioning it out secretly to people. But now that prophet talked about the next million that was coming in.

I have this chapter about unbelieving believers because it does not make sense to be one. If you had Jesus tell you, "Listen, I got this taken care of if you will go back and tell people the truth about Me." Jesus is so misrepresented. I saw things in Heaven that some people might have a problem with; for instance, I have a gold driveway there. Someone here might be mad because I do not have a gravel one. After all, it is such a waste of gold. What is waste in Heaven? There is nothing in Heaven that is below standard. Gravel is here on earth because we are in a fallen world.

Jesus would not let me talk about my heavenly experience for twenty-three years, and I did not. So I got to teach a Sunday school class, and instead of flying the airplane, I got to be a flight attendant. I lived my life like this and kept living it until there was nothing left of me. After twenty-three years, all of a sudden, Jesus appeared to me and told me it was time to write the book. Kathi came and told me that she got the same briefing that Jesus gave me, and with Kathi's confirmation, I wrote the book.

What will switch on you is that you cannot fail when you realize that the limits have been taken off! I am not just saying this to make you feel better, because I have no reason to do any of this because I do not need anything. I legitimately saw that God really does favor His people, and He loves His people. God wants to trust you, and if you can pass your test, God will start putting responsibility onto you to where you will be able to run with the horses. If you can be trusted with little, you can be trusted with much (see Luke 16:10), including great wealth. God will trust you with kingdoms and angels.

I already saw the future, and that is all going to happen. I can even tell you what I will be wearing, and when you see me, you will say, "Hey, you talked about your uniform." I had an ambassador's uniform made of pure rose gold. Some people might be mad because it is such a waste, and I should have gotten polyester. But it doesn't matter, and it was beautiful rose gold. Jesus was not nervous about my wearing gold because it might wrinkle if I sat down in it. When we went from room to room in Heaven, Jesus never asked me if I could turn the lights off because they were trying to save money.

I will do what the Lord wants me to do no matter what it costs me, even if I have to do it for free. I have told the Lord that I will go back to work if I have to, even though I have already worked 30 years at one company. I have worked since I was 14 years old because I had to pay for rent and food while I was going to high school. I would have to go to my grandma's so I could get enough to eat. My family was very big, and they could not always afford food. There were times when I did not get to eat, and that is why I like to buy people's meals today. I do not want anyone to have to go through what I went through because it is not God's will. Prosperity is good as long as you use it correctly. Prosperity is to be used to set people free and to help people.

> *In this manner, therefore, pray: Our Father in Heaven, hallowed be Your name. Your kingdom come. Your will be done on earth as it is in heaven.*
> —MATTHEW 6:9-10

Here we are bringing what is in Heaven down to the earth. There is healing in Heaven, but there is no sickness. There is abundance, and there is no poverty. There is no lack in the kingdom of God. I am not going to go around giving out lack, but I will be going about doing good and healing everyone just like Jesus did. I will be giving out from the other kingdom, and I will distribute what is in Heaven onto the earth. That is what changes lives, and it transforms them.

CHARACTER OVER COMFORT

> *Therefore, indeed, I send you prophets, wise men, and scribes: some of them you will kill and crucify, and some of them you will scourge in your synagogues and persecute from city to city.*
> —MATTHEW 23:34

They always want to kill the prophets in the generation they live in, but afterward they celebrate them as heroes. Prophets usually speak correction to their generation, but it is not discerned until later. By then, often, destruction occurs because although people are warned to listen to what is being said, they do not adhere to the Word of the Lord. There are consequences for not listening to God's Word through His prophets.

I saw that many people in this generation are going to be saved. They are going to be rerouted and put in the right place because God is having His way. There is a perspective in Heaven that is far beyond our comprehension, and it takes a person coming back and speaking from that realm. I have been told that other people will be sent back from Heaven and have the same kind of story as I do. At the end of this age, there will be these kinds of stories coming forth to reroute people and bring them into a place where they are walking correctly with the Lord. Revelation needs to come up several notches more.

We have been neutralized because we have backed off on the Word of God to accommodate the inactivity of God because of our disobedience and our unbelief. To keep a large church, you have to accommodate people, and you have to do certain things to keep them. If you tell them the truth, they might not want the truth because they want to feel comfortable. Jesus said to me, "I am more concerned about your character than I am about your comfort." I went through things to be a carrier of the glory because my character would be the carrier.

You can go to a meeting and get blasted by the Holy Spirit to where they have to carry you out, and it has happened to me. However, you cannot walk in that man's or woman's anointing because you do not have the character to hold it and carry it as that person has had to learn. You can experience a ministry gift and then wonder what happens Monday morning when they are on an airplane leaving, and you are left with all your devils. They have come back to harass you, and you are not quite ready to handle them.

One of the reasons to immerse people in kingdom teaching is to transform them by the Word of the Lord. When I was in Heaven, I told the Lord that I want the change in people to be permanent if I come back, and I did not want it to leak out. I want people's experience to be permanent.

> *How God anointed Jesus of Nazareth with the Holy Spirit and with power, who went about doing good and healing all who were oppressed by the devil, for God was with Him.*
>
> —ACTS 10:38

It should be permanent because the Word of God is true, and the Spirit of God is the Spirit of Truth. Jesus, when God anointed Him, went around doing good and healing everyone who was oppressed by the devil, so that is God's will. Once we get into the authority, unbelief just leaves us because we are submitted to authority, and that is when provision comes. We no longer have to concentrate on provision because we are walking in it, and you rest in it.

> *You've gone into my future to prepare the way, and in kindness you follow behind me to spare me from the harm of my past. You have laid your hand on me!*
>
> —PSALM 139:5 TPT

This Scripture reflects the Jesus I met, and He has already made the pathway to my future, and He is standing on it waiting for me to come to Him. Then He protects me from the harm of my past, and He lays His hand on me and imparts to me the Father's blessing.

In John 17, Jesus told the disciples that He was going back to the Father. He prayed and said that He had glorified the Father and done everything He had been asked to do. Jesus explained that He would be going back to the Father and the glory that He had before the worlds were formed. Then Jesus prayed for His disciples and for all of those who would believe in Him. Jesus prayed, "Holy Father, protect them by the power of Your name, the name You gave Me, so that they may be one as We are one" (see John 17:11). John 17 was what Jesus prayed for us, and I guarantee you that He is going to get the answer to His prayer, and you are a product of that prayer.

You are going to experience the glory, you are going to experience the unity, and you are going to experience the love of God through Jesus' prayer. If God is for you, who can be against you? (See Romans 8:31.) Paul started writing Romans 8 with, *"There is therefore now no condemnation to those who are in Christ Jesus"* (Rom. 8:1). Then Paul talks about how those who walk in the Spirit please God, and those who do not walk in the Spirit cannot please God (see Rom. 8:4-10). Paul is walking you through Romans 8.

In Romans 8:15, Paul says, "We have been given the Spirit of adoption." The word that is used for *adoption* there is *acceptance*. We are accepted in the beloved. At the end of Romans 8, Paul asks, *"Who shall separate us from the love of Christ? ...Yet in all these things we are more than conquerors through Him who loved us"* (Rom. 8:35,37).

> *I know how to be abased, and I know how to abound. Everywhere and in all things I have learned both to be full and to be hungry, both to abound and to suffer need. I can do all things through Christ who strengthens me.*
> —PHILIPPIANS 4:12-13

Paul walks you through Romans 8 because he was caught up to Heaven, and he saw the frailty of man, but he also saw the power of God, the provision, and the whole covenant of God. He never let anything shake him because he knew that he was one with God. Paul said, *"For to me, to live is Christ, and to die is gain"* (Phil. 1:21).

There is a cloud of witnesses in Heaven, and they are waiting for us to finish our part. They would want you to know that you do not have to doubt, and you do not have to fear that it is already set up. They have done their part, and it was a big part, and now they are cheering us on, and they all want us to succeed. You do not have to yield to the works of the flesh. You do not have to yield to the mind's way of doing things if it is not correct.

You must be careful about what you see and hear because it can very powerfully influence you. I will tell you why—your mind and your body follow your thoughts. Your mind follows thoughts that produce emotions and produce chemicals in your body. Your mind cannot discern truth unless truth has already been put into it as a standard. If you see something, your mind will automatically process it as real, even if it is a familiar spirit. Your mind will start to picture what you are seeing, and then your body will produce chemicals to have a feeling and make it something real.

When I was little, I imagined what it would be like to have a million dollars because we were so poor. I would sit in first and second grade, and I would imagine what it would be like to have a million dollars and what I would do with it. When someone gave my wife and me a million dollars, I experienced the same feeling I had in second grade when I pictured getting it. There was no difference, and that is how powerful your imagination is. Your body just follows with what you think, and that is why you are what you think. You must have a standard other than your born-again spirit to keep yourself in line with the truth. You have to frame your world with the *Word of God* as truth and measure everything by it.

> *As His divine power has given to us all things that pertain to life and godliness, through the knowledge of Him who called us by glory and virtue, by which have been given to us exceedingly great and precious promises, that through these you may be partakers of the divine nature, having escaped the corruption that is in the world through lust.*
> —2 PETER 1:3-4

I am telling you, what I saw in Heaven was that we were given everything we need for life and godliness and that we can be partakers of the divine nature, and that is what gets rid of our unbelief and wavering.

Chapter 5

TURNING THE TABLES ON THE ENEMY

But if you indeed obey His voice and do all that I speak, then I will be an enemy to your enemies and an adversary to your adversaries.

—Exodus 23:22

T HE ENEMY WILL put poison in front of you to poison you. Then he will sit there and drink something that does not have poison in it, and he will say, "Okay, let's have a drink." And you are thinking, *Something is wrong here*, so you turn the table on the enemy. Now the enemy has your glass in front of him, and he gets really nervous, and you say, "Okay, let's drink!"

Suddenly, you see a stress crack because now the devil will have to drink his own poison. That is what I mean by turning the tables on the enemy.

In Exodus 23:22, it says, *"If you indeed obey His voice and do all that I speak, then I will be an enemy to your enemies and an adversary to your adversaries."* God has already proclaimed that your enemies are His enemies, and it is part of the covenant.

I never wanted to work where I ended up working for 30 years. I certainly did not want to be in the airplane cabin if I could be in the cockpit. Once I got into the cabin as a flight attendant, I especially did not want to be there. You cannot imagine what that job entails. I used to go into the lavatory every flight and say, "God, whatever I have done to offend You, I am so sorry."

When I graduated from Rhema Bible College, I was asked to stay with the college and travel as a singer for Rhema with Brother Hagin. I prayed, and the Lord told me not to do it, so I went to the airline. I had graduated and was fully capable of being in the ministry. I had donated one year after I graduated from school to help the youth at Rhema. Even though I worked at the church for free, I worked extra hard.

When I was asked to be a singer, I was very excited until the Lord said, "You are going to go to Southwest Airlines, and I told you this a while back." I said, "Okay, Lord, I guess being a pilot is alright." The Lord said, "Oh, no, not a pilot. You are going to be a flight attendant." I thought, *What have I done?* The thing about it is, what I went through at my job prepared me for what I am doing now.

You might not believe this, but the only reason I can do what I am doing right now in my life is because of that job. I could never get up in front of people and speak or do anything, let alone play instruments and sing. I teach college classes and write books, and I can do all these different things all because I was placed in a situation where I was very uncomfortable, and it was not part of my personality.

I have had everything in the Bible and some things that are not in the Bible happen to me. I have seen things, and I have encountered things that I did not think were possible. I thought that Sodom and Gomorrah had been destroyed, and then I worked on an airplane, and it was a free-for-all. I had an education and visitations from Jesus, but it did not stop many people from trying to get me fired. Throughout my career, 21 people have tried to get me fired.

I would get pulled in for drinking on the job or stealing money, and I would say, "I am a minister, you know that, and I do not drink. I have never had a beer, and I work for a living. I do not need to steal." Finally, management asked, "Kevin, what is going on?" I told them, "They are asking me to drink with them at night, and I don't drink. They want me to go to bed with them, and I don't do that because I am a minister." I was not even married yet, and I could have done what I wanted, but I always walked away from it. When I was eventually married, I was faithful to my wife, my whole marriage.

These kinds of problems are real and happen to godly men and women in their jobs all of the time. All of these people who tried to get me fired ended up getting fired themselves, and some people who ended up doing terrible things against us are dead now. I did not have anything to do with it, but I felt bad for them when they were doing the things they were doing. I remember thinking, *This will not go well*, because I could almost hear the sword of the Lord being drawn.

There is going to come a time when you will hear the sword being drawn. It has happened to me even recently that I heard that sword being drawn, and that Jesus was done. I do whatever Jesus tells me to do, but then I tell the other party that I am sorry, it is out of my hands now, and it is not going to be pretty. The Word of the Lord will come to me in these situations and tell me the truth about something, and the other party does not know that I know the truth. I hear conversations that they have in secret.

I tell you this because when the tables are turned, what happens is that God starts to protect you and treat you with respect and honor. If people start to dishonor you, it is only a matter of time before you will hear a sword being pulled out of a sheath.

> *Beloved, do not avenge yourselves, but rather give*
> *place to wrath; for it is written, "Vengeance is Mine,*
> *I will repay," says the Lord.*
> —ROMANS 12:19

When something happens, you just step back, and you know that it is out of your hands now, and you can only watch what happens. I have watched good people get disqualified because they went too far. The tables are turned on the enemy, but now people must begin to honor and respect the church's fivefold offices. They have to honor each other and walk in love toward one another, and if they do not there is another side of God that they do not want to meet. I have seen people meet that side of God. Some people do not even believe that God can be that way, and then they end up on the wrong side.

> *Do not be deceived, God is not mocked; for whatever a man sows, that he will also reap. For he who sows to his flesh will of the flesh reap corruption, but he who sows to the Spirit will of the Spirit reap everlasting life. And let us not grow weary while doing good, for in due season we shall reap if we do not lose heart.*
>
> —GALATIANS 6:7-9

You reap what you sow, and God is not mocked, which means that whatever you sow, you will reap. If you are sowing toward destruction, that is what you reap. If you are sowing into the flesh, you will reap the flesh; this is true for everyone. You need to stay clean and be careful not to come against the body of Christ. Jesus specifically said, *"Anyone who speaks a word against the Son of Man, it will be forgiven him; but whoever speaks against the Holy Spirit, it will not be forgiven him, either in this age or in the age to come"* (Matt. 12:32). There are a lot of things happening to people, and it is because they have come against the Holy Spirit.

If God tells you to do something and someone tries to stop you from doing it, God has to judge between you and them. If God speaks to you and tells you to do something and another person resists that, who are they trying to stop? God. If you are being persecuted, if you are being mistreated, there has to come a point where God has to judge between you and that person.

You may be overwhelmed and overburdened with things that have happened to you. What you have not done is rightly discerned that the tables have been turned, and so you are beating yourself up. Jesus told me that it would be better for those who came against Him to have a millstone tied around their neck than to offend a little one like me (see Luke 17:2). God is protective over me. Jesus said to me that it would have been better for the one who would betray me if they had never been born. Well, that does not sound like a God of love. Do you see how much we have to mature?

SET APART AS SONS AND DAUGHTERS

For the Lord disciplines those he loves, and he punishes each one he accepts as his child.
—HEBREWS 12:6 NLT

This Scripture is not this generation's definition of love. However, when God disciplines those He loves, He is treating you as sons and daughters. When the tables turn, Paul said, *"and being ready to punish all disobedience when your obedience is fulfilled"* (2 Cor. 10:6). When your obedience is established first, then the Holy Spirit can come in and make it right.

Come out from among them and be separate, says the Lord. Do not touch what is unclean, and I will

*receive you. I will be a Father to you, and you shall
be My sons and daughters, says the Lord Almighty.*
—2 CORINTHIANS 6:17-18

*For if we would judge ourselves, we would not be
judged. But when we are judged, we are chastened
by the Lord, that we may not be condemned with
the world.*
—1 CORINTHIANS 11:31-32

Paul said to come out and be separate from among them, be
holy, separate, set apart. You have to pull yourself away like that
because when judgment comes, you do not want to be included
in that. You do not want to be judged like the world is going to
be judged. You separate yourself from the world, and you judge
yourself so that you will not be judged.

*Then Moses went up, also Aaron, Nadab, and
Abihu, and seventy of the elders of Israel, and they
saw the God of Israel. And there was under His feet
as it were a paved work of sapphire stone, and it was
like the very heavens in its clarity.*
—EXODUS 24:9-10

I saw that even though God is perfect and holy, when He
came down and He stood before Moses and the 70 elders and ate
in front of them, He did not judge Israel. At that time, God was
mad at the Israelites, but He stood back, and He did not judge
them. God let them come halfway up the mountain with Moses,

and then He let them eat there. God Himself stood on that sapphire stone platform.

I saw this sapphire stone in Heaven. It is the flooring in the throne room of God, and white flames were coming up through the stones. It is beautiful, but it is very, very holy. Not everyone can walk on it because it is something that you must be invited to do. I did not get to walk on it at first until Jesus explained that it had nothing to do with position and everything to do with the relationship that you have with the Lord. Only people who had walked in the fear of the Lord and in a relationship with Him could walk on those sapphire stones amidst the flames.

WALKING IN AND BEING UNDER AUTHORITY

While I was standing there with Jesus, He mentioned individuals you would know. He mentioned Moses and David, but then He mentioned Lester Sumrall. Jesus said that He mentioned him because Lester Sumrall had developed his spirit to the place where it expanded out to affect a whole city when he entered it. Jesus said, "Yours, Kevin, is about 30 feet." He told me that the whole city would come under Lester's authority in Christ when he entered it. Demons would leave so that they would not be cast out, and they could come back later. I saw Lester going into San Francisco, and all the demons were alerted that he was coming in, and they were getting out of his way. He had already upended Manila, and the news got around.

These are the kinds of things that happen when you walk in the authority of God. Another thing that might happen is you might lose your friends because they will start mistreating you. They might just go away, or they might start acting out around you. The reason is that they have invisible friends. I am serious.

Jesus reminded me of how Paul was shipwrecked on the island of Malta. He told me that when Paul gathered up the fire-wood on the beach, the viper did not come out until he laid the wood on the fire. Do you realize that Paul picked all that wood up and walked down the beach, and everything was fine until he got it close to the fire and the fire exposed the viper? The Lord said, "When things get real hot with the fire, the vipers are going to come out."

As the fire in your life increases, do not be surprised or concerned when your friends start freaking out. You need to realize that the vipers were always there, only you had airbrushed them out of the picture. The Lord said, "That is a problem with you, Kevin—you airbrush to make people fit when they do not, and it comes back to bite you." You can judge people incorrectly because you love them and want to give them a chance, but the truth is that a viper will always be a viper. As an apostle, a true father, Paul made decisions knowing that he had to protect the flock, which pastors do. Pastors know that a wolf in sheep's clothing will not go well, and a wolf is never going to be a sheep because he is a wolf.

I have a friend in our ministry, and every time I am at his house, his dog just loves me and lays by my feet. Whenever we would sit and talk, I would pet the dog, and the dog just loved it. They cannot believe how much their dog loves me, considering that I am a stranger.

One day, as we were talking about the ministry's future and having a serious staff meeting, I do not know why, but I stopped petting the dog. The dog tried to get my attention, and then it got up and strutted off to the middle of the room, turned around and looked at me, and went "Grarrre" and walked out. Everyone burst out laughing, and I did not know it, but she had just broken up with me, and now she's done with me. Why? Because I would not do what that dog wanted me to do. That is what happens with control. Jezebel uses rejection, and Ahab sides with her because he is weak.

When we had horses, my horse wanted to be the boss. In the pecking order, he was trying to make himself the alpha male. Whenever I got around him, he would turn around and try to bite me, as he did to everyone to prove that he is in authority. You can either submit or fight. I had to establish my authority. Every time he would turn around and bite me, the Lord told me to reach up and pinch him. He would look at me, and the next time he would think twice.

The devil is trying to get you to submit, and you must establish your authority in Christ. People driven by devils and controlled by devils will try to get you to submit. They want to rule over you, but the last time I checked, I am free in Christ.

I have a pastor, and she is a woman, and she is a good pastor. When I was without a pastor, I went through a lot of warfare that I no longer experience with a pastor. I learned to get under authority. It is the way that God set it up. There is a pecking order. There is a way that things are in the spirit, and demons need to be treated roughly.

God has to have a sapphire platform to come onto the earth. The earth is cursed, and it would break apart if God touched it. The voice of the Lord breaks the cedars and they splinter (see Ps. 29:5). When God speaks, there is thunder and lightning (see Job 37:2-5). The mountains melt like wax at the presence of the Lord (see Ps. 97:5). All of these things happen because the world is not the way God made it. It is a fallen world, and so it cannot handle God.

When I was in Heaven, I saw that we were created to handle God. If we look at God's face in our earthly bodies, our body will melt because you cannot live if you see God in the flesh. However, you can live in Heaven and see Him. I do not believe anyone who has said they have seen the face of God. In Heaven, I was told if I looked at the face of the Father I could not go back because my body could not handle it. Your earthly body is fallen.

I have had a lot of angels come, and none of them had wings. The Bible says that the winged creatures are in the throne room of God. There are the living creatures (see Rev. 4:8), the cherubim (see Ezek. 10:5), and the seraphim (see Isa. 6:2). Jesus gave us authority over earthbound devils, serpents, and scorpions, the ones that are on the ground (see Luke 10:19). *"Yet Michael the archangel, in contending with the devil, when he disputed about the body of Moses, dared not bring against him a reviling accusation, but said, 'The Lord rebuke you!'"* (Jude 1:9). Michael, the archangel, did not rebuke the devil because he understood authority. In the Bible, lucifer—whose name is *hillel* in Hebrew, which means the bright and shiny one—is one of the cherubim. He is a cherub and not an archangel (see Ezek. 28:14).

Archangels do not need wings, and they actually run right into the air. They are so fast that light stretches behind them when they come in. When an angel comes into a meeting, it will be like a flash because he is coming in faster than light, and the light stretches. When the angel stops, the light piles up, and it comes in. You have to be ready when that happens, but they do not need wings. The angels with wings are to protect the assets of God.

In God's throne room, the seraphim are protecting themselves. The cherubim are protecting everyone else around the throne from the glory coming from the face of the Father. There is a cherub on each side of the Father with wings that cover Him. *"He shall cover you with His feathers, and under His wings you shall take refuge"* (Ps. 91:4). In this psalm, the cherubim are the ones that have the wings, not God. God does not have wings; the psalmist is describing the wings of the cherubim. God spoke to Moses and told him to make the mercy seat and gave Moses very precise specifications to build the ark of the covenant. It is an exact replica of what is in Heaven, including the cherubim (see Exod. 25:10-22).

Now that you have decided to let the tables turn on the enemy, what happens is that now you will find yourself in charge. Suddenly everything will become clear to you, including binding and loosing and the keys to the kingdom. Jesus said, *"If you for-give the sins of any, they are forgiven them; if you retain the sins of any, they are retained"* (John 20:23). He also said that if you go to a place and they do not accept you, then take your peace back and leave (see Matt. 10:13-14). When the tables turn, then you are in charge, and now the devil will have to listen to what you say. Are you ready for that kind of showdown? All of a sudden, the enemy is on the run.

> *Therefore submit to God. Resist the devil and he*
> *will flee from you.*
>
> —James 4:7

It says here that you must first submit to God, which is talking about being under authority, and then you resist the devil. The word *resist* is when you *push back*. If a policeman is trying to arrest you and you decide to *push back*, you are resisting arrest, and then you get another count against you. Now you have two things going on, two different court dates—one for the crime you were pulled over for and a second one for resisting arrest. So if you submit to God and *push back* against the devil, he will flee from you. The same word is used here. *"God resists the proud, but gives grace to the humble"* (1 Pet. 5:5). It is the same word used here—*push back*. God pushes back the prideful. Being prideful does not pay good dividends, and it is not a good investment at all.

You are going to have to be more aggressive and be able to get rough with the devil. You have to be rough with him because you cannot give him any rest. The Lord told me to take a two by four to the devil every morning. The reason He told me that was because the Lord knew that I loved the cartoon Foghorn Leghorn. He was a rooster, and no matter who he was talking to, he would ask them to wait a minute. Then for no reason at all, Foghorn would go and get that two by four and go into the doghouse and just beat the living daylights out of that dog. The dog would be so traumatized that he would take his leash and put it on the clothesline himself. The Lord said to me, "That's how you have to treat the devil. You just give him his daily beating."

Some people actually say to me, "You are not treating the devil with respect. You should not be talking like that." I say, "So you are his lawyer?" What church do you go to? You have to be rough with the devil. He had no problem being rough with you and tormenting you and your loved ones. Don't you think it is his time to take the poison that he has been feeding you to try to kill you? Isn't it about time that the tables are turned?

The body of Christ needs to take the authority that has already been given to them. Jesus would come down here and say, "I already instructed you to use My name." Jesus is not going to drive out the devils because He has given all the keys to the king-dom to the Church (see Matt. 16:19). Then Jesus went and was seated at the right hand of God, and He is sitting there waiting for His enemies to be made His footstool (see Heb. 10:12-13).

We are to bring the head of the enemy and place it under Jesus' feet. In the past, a king would put his feet on his enemy's severed head to show complete domination. When they would take over a kingdom, they would place the head of the dead king at the throne. The conquering king would then put his feet on top of the head as a sign of full authority. That is what Paul was saying there.

TIME FOR OVERTHROW!

The problem is that for some Christians, that is too much for Christianity these days. No wonder we are getting beat up with the things that we are encountering. People are getting all kinds of things happening to them, and what they are telling me is beyond my comprehension. Right now, we need to be prepared to be the ones in charge down here. Until the harvest comes in, Jesus is not coming back. When I pray, when I intercede, I do not even pray for myself. There will come a day when you will not need to pray for yourself, and you will be praying for others. It is time for overthrow.

> *No evil shall befall you, nor shall any plague come near your dwelling; for He shall give His angels charge over you, to keep you in all your ways. In their hands they shall bear you up, lest you dash your foot against a stone.*
> —PSALM 91:10-12

If you make the Most High your dwelling place, all of these benefits are yours. It says nothing evil can touch you, and no disease can touch you. Somebody has got to stand up for God and say, "Something is wrong here!" If it is not happening, it is not God's fault because He has already promised this to us.

Chapter 6

THE ENEMY WITHIN

*In meekness instructing those that oppose themselves;
if God peradventure will give them repentance to
the acknowledging of the truth; and that they may
recover themselves out of the snare of the devil, who
are taken captive by him at his will.*
— 2 Timothy 2:25-26 KJV

HAVE YOU EVER noticed that people around you sometimes work against themselves? We need edges trimmed off of us all the time, and we are not always where we should be because we are being formed into His image. Even though we have God's plan, we do not always understand it, so we do not always implement it. We need help, and we need people who are just brave enough to preach the whole Gospel so that we can all develop. There are things that people will not talk about, and one of them is that we can oppose ourselves within ourselves.

We are always arguing about whether a Christian can have a demon or if a demon can have a Christian, but I would want to be someone who is known in hell. When you are known in hell, the word gets around, and demons start to leave before you get there. They get notified that you are coming, and they know who you are. It gets around that you are someone who knows who they are in Christ, you know what is going on, and you know how to take care of things. If you have established your authority, the demons want to opt out. You know that you are under authority, and you have authority.

Demons know if a Christian is not sure of who they are in Christ. A demon is like a horse, and they know if you know what you are doing or not. You do not even have to get on a horse because they instinctively know when you approach them if you have authority. If you do not know what you are doing, they will take advantage of you. If you do not establish your authority, they will take you for a ride instead of you taking them for a ride.

A car does not stay on the road because you are in the driver's seat. You still have to do some things yourself. It is the same with the life of a Christian, and it does not work by default. The world is constantly changing around you in the spirit realm, and you have to be smart. One of the subjects that can help you take off the limitations is talking about who you are and how things work inside you.

There are different parts of you, and I can appeal to your flesh, appeal to your emotions, or appeal to your spirit. Now, this may shock you, but most church activity takes place in the soul realm. It is not in the spirit realm at all, and because of that you feel good, even though you waited three hours to go through a fire tunnel, but the next morning you wake up and it is gone, and you need another one. Jesus never set up any fire tunnels for the disciples to go through, and the early church did not have fire tunnels either.

> *Therefore be imitators of God as dear children. And walk in love, as Christ also has loved us and given Himself for us, an offering and a sacrifice to God for a sweet-smelling aroma.*
> —EPHESIANS 5:1-2

When I get in a situation, the bottom line is that I want to know how to handle myself. I want to operate correctly and in a way that pleases God. I want to be one of those people whom Heaven can trust. Do you want to be on that list? You can think of certain people who, when you call them, will be there for you. They are the ones who can help you, but there are very few of them because they do not make people like that anymore. They are people whom you can depend upon when you need help, and they are there for you, but you are there for them, too. So there is an exchange.

I have noticed in Christianity that people do not know how to deal with spiritual activity when it happens to them. Now when something happens to me, I go over it and investigate it and ask myself questions. "I feel irritated right now. Why?" I discovered something early in my Christian walk before I was ever on the other side in Heaven. I noticed that as I would fall asleep and fall through into the outer reaches of a deep sleep, I could see into the spiritual realm. There was a point where my spirit man could turn and look, and I could see into the spirit realm for only a flash before I would fall asleep.

Sometimes I would see someone standing there or hear a devil screaming at the top of its lungs. It was just for a second, and it happened many times. Later on, when I was on the other side, I saw that the reason you might feel irritated is that there is a demonic spirit screaming at you, harassing you, and talking trash to you. You can start to feel stress in your body, and if your body starts to go with it and you do not do anything about it, you will need medication. I saw this in Heaven.

I noticed that I might feel a power in prayer or feel fire near me, and I know that is my angel. It was different from when I went to sleep, and I would see a fiery figure standing there as I fell asleep. I realized my feelings were because there was an evil entity that I could not see in the natural. It was causing me to have feelings or thoughts, and it was either good or evil. I started to discern that people do not know what I found out, and they need to know.

DISCERNING THE SPIRIT REALM

People need to understand that there are different parts of them. There is your *mind*, which includes your *will* and *emotions,* and they are all tied up together in the psychological part of you. You can go through counseling, and someone who is trained in this can help you sort through things psychologically so that they can lay it out before you. That can help you deal with some things and answer questions on why you react a certain way, and that person can help you walk through things.

However, there may come the point in counseling when there can be something spiritual going on, too. Sometimes a spiritual thing transfers over into the psychological and the emotional and then over into the physical. If you take medication, it will only take away the symptoms. You could be opposing yourself from within yourself because of a demonic influence that you do not understand or know.

You do not know why you feel something every time you go to the bus stop and stand right by that bench. If you could see in the spirit, you would see that there was a demon entity that is assigned right there to harass every person who is waiting for the bus. If I had not told you this, you would not have understood that this is what they do. Now I know their favorite places are in grocery stores and shopping malls, and they traffic themselves there. They go there, and they wait to assign themselves to people, and when you walk into the grocery store, you will feel all kinds of stuff because there are spirits everywhere.

I do not go shopping that much anymore, and most things I get on Amazon now. Once you get to a certain place in the Spirit, you do not want to get knocked out of that because you will become very sensitive. If I am around very needy people, then I want to help them. If I am not supposed to help them, or if I cannot help them, then I have to wait for the power of God to come upon me and administer by the Word of the Lord, or I have to opt out. I must be very careful to be led by the Holy Spirit, or I could be praying for people all the time, and they would not be receiving from God as they should.

> *But He was wounded for our transgressions, He was bruised for our iniquities; the chastisement for our peace was upon Him, and by His stripes we are healed.*
> —ISAIAH 53:5

Some people can experience the power of God and never seek God or transform their minds by the Word of God, and then they come back the next year, and everything is still the same. I ask them, "Didn't I pray for you last year? What happened?" There has to come a time when you graduate, and God comes through for you because He is not mocked, and a man is going to reap what he sows (see Gal. 6:7). There has to be something else going on, and it is a demon entity, and everyone has to learn how to walk in their authority.

You can oppose yourself within yourself; the apostle Paul spoke about this in Second Timothy 2:24-26. That would mean that we have to have different parts of us. We would have to have a soul, and we would have to have a spirit. So the heart of man, the spirit of man is born again. However, the soul is not saved, and it needs to be renewed. Your soul, which is your *mind, will,* and *emotions,* needs to be taught how to respond. Unfortunately, these parts of you can easily be affected by spiritual entities.

> *Jesus said to him, "I am the way, the truth, and the life. No one comes to the Father except through Me."*
> —JOHN 14:6

*You used to live in sin, just like the rest of the world,
obeying the devil—the commander of the powers
in the unseen world. He is the spirit at work in the
hearts of those who refuse to obey God.*

—Ephesians 2:2 NLT

Man was made in the image of God (see Gen. 1:27), and that means that even fallen man is still better than any demon spirit. However, in order to have power over demons, you have to be saved and born again. You cannot simply resist demon spirits. Paul said the people in the world cannot resist the spirit of the air, and they are slaves to it. Any unsaved person can be infiltrated and used against what God is doing on the earth because they have no resistance to the spirit of the air. A Christian should not be infiltrated, but evil spirits will come around you and try to convince you that you are "this or that." If you are not careful, you will start to think it is you.

It is important for believers to come to church, come to services, be around people, and not be isolated. Isolation can cause people to feel rejected, and satan can use that, and it is how he works. The devil can feel their rejection and uses it. You may be feeling rejected and not know why. Feelings are supposed to be for adding to the experience of the Spirit. You are supposed to experience things in the Spirit, and then your soul adds to it. It is not supposed to be the other way around, where you feel first from the soul realm.

If you are not careful, you could go to church and feel something, but it could be a soulish thing and not a spiritual experience. However, going to church is supposed to be a spiritual experience, and your soul is supposed to add to that feeling. When you have something happen to you in the Spirit, your soul adds to it, and you have feelings and emotions. Happiness is an emotion that we have down here on earth, but joy is in Heaven. Joy is a spiritual experience, whereas happiness can come and go.

Truth is always going to be truth, even if it evades you on a certain subject. Truth is out there, and it is available to you in the Spirit. If you feel dumb or stupid, you are not, and it just means that you need to go into a deeper revelation, which you can find in a spiritual experience. Revelation comes from your spirit, which is inside of you. Now, *"God is Spirit, and those who worship Him must worship Him in spirit and truth"* (John 4:24). God is going to talk to you through your spirit. God gave you a mind and body, but they are supposed to follow your spirit, that inner part of you.

Here is how satan gets you to oppose yourself. God lays out the truth, and He does not defend Himself. When I was in Heaven and Jesus was speaking to me, I did not say very much because I wanted to let Him talk the whole time. I knew that I did not know what Jesus knows, and I did not want to stop Him from talking. I knew I needed to hear what He was saying.

Jesus never tried to defend Himself, and it occurred to me that He was earnestly trying to help me until I realized that He was really trying to help you. After 45 minutes, it began to dawn on me that He was not talking about Heaven at all because Jesus was talking about how to live down here on earth, which I did not need anymore. Then I did the math and concluded that I was going back, but I did not want to go back! I felt bewildered and thought I had really messed up. It was my fault, but I did not grasp the truth, and I was opposing myself.

I saw that only 20 percent of the activity was spiritual in church services, but we call it spiritual. For instance, I can talk to you and make you feel good, or I could tug on your emotions, and you could give to me. I could tell you a sad story about how I needed money, and before you know it, most people would be moved to help me. That is called manipulation, and I would be afraid of going to hell if I used it. I have the fear of the Lord, and I would never do that.

Did you know that in some of the revivals in the 1950s, they learned how to take offerings as soon as someone got healed to play off of people's emotions? There might be ten offerings in one night to play off the fact that God had healed someone. That is not a spiritual experience, but it is manipulation in the soul realm. Why does God always ask for a $1,000 offering? Why is it always an even number? Why isn't it a Scripture verse? Something like $19.10 for Isaiah 19:10. We get used to this kind of activity, and then when God sneezes, we have a revival because He just accidentally sneezed. Oh my goodness, did you feel that?

God is supposed to be able to move freely among us all the time. We should walk into the realms of Heaven in a room where we meet, and it should be free of demons. We should not have to do an hour of worship. We should do it because we want to, but we should not have to do what I call "a car wash" if we do not. You should not have to go through an hour car wash after being out there in the world just to get in the frame of mind to receive the Word of God. It should not be that way. You should walk into a church service and be ready, but we have to worship, which is fine because we can worship.

I saw that I could walk in and start teaching, and I tested it. I am walking in because of my own personal relationship, and like you I do not need music. The ministry gift will start to slice through the air, and we do not have to work you up. That was why Paul said that when you come into a meeting, predetermine what you will give without compulsion, for God loves a cheerful giver (see 2 Cor. 9:7).

God wants you to give, but He does not want you to give under duress or give out of pressure. You should determine what you want to give in your heart, and you should act according to your faith. Give what God has already put inside of you, and if you understand, you cannot lose. If you do not allow the spiritual activity to happen in your life, you will not discern whose voice you hear. You will not be able to tell if it is the Holy Spirit, your spirit, an angel of God, or a demon spirit.

There are all these different voices going on around you, and I have seen all these things. It is real, but no one wants to talk about it, and everyone seems to bear it the way it is. You go home, feeling lonely and rejected, and have things harassing you at night, and you cannot figure out why you do not fit in. It is a little too late for you to tell me that God does not heal everyone because I have two brand-new kidneys, and I do not wear glasses anymore. My optometrist says this does not happen, and he has never seen it before. Someone who is almost 60 years old does not need their glasses or contacts anymore.

ADVANCEMENT OF THE KINGDOM THROUGH YOU

I have had things happen to me. You cannot preach to me about healing or God wanting to bless you because it is a little too late for me. If you have heard my stories, it was when I stopped seeking money that it started seeking me out and tackling me. The kingdom will advance at a huge rate through people who will let God overcome them and convince them. He wins you over, but what you have got to do is to not oppose yourself within yourself.

You need to find out what God is saying concerning you about every area of your life. You have got to get rid of the controversies. There are people I know who had a traumatic event happen when they were a child, and they are stuck there and they live out of that age. They never mature, and I encounter it all the time. It is a demon that entraps people, and God did not do that to you. I have had terrible things happen to me. I have had to resolve my heart and mind that this happened because I live in a fallen and broken world.

I knew that God loved me, but I was not operating in the fullness of what I am operating in now. Once I had an understanding of God's ways, I would not allow certain things to happen. I do not find myself in situations because I do not go there. I do not allow myself to be pulled into situations because I can see them developing, and I now know not to go there.

I will just tell people, "I am not going to do that today." Or, "I am not going to go there because I am going to have to go this way because this is what the Lord is saying." Everyone has to be ready to move with that because it is based on revelation. I do not know everything, and neither do you, but when God does speak you have to go with it. God might be outfoxing the devil because the devil was standing there waiting for you at the intersection, but the Holy Spirit had you go another way.

Some things are set up to hurt you and slander God to you and make it look like God is not protecting you. It is made to look random like it is just what happens. It is never God's will for certain things to happen, but they do happen. There has to be a part of you that agrees with God at times like that.

> *Why am I discouraged? Why is my heart so sad? I*
> *will put my hope in God! I will praise him again—*
> *my Savior and my God!*
> —Psalm 42:11 NLT

David said, "Hope in God; for I shall yet praise Him." When things happened, David knew how to trust God and speak to himself and encourage himself in the Lord. That means that there are different parts of you. You need to get on the same page as God, and you need to know His ways, the way *He* likes to do things. Then you will start to see a transformation in your life, and you begin to realize that this is how God chooses to do things. The enemy does not understand God's ways.

Hillel was one of God's cherubim, and in English his name is translated lucifer, but in Hebrew it is hillel. When hillel was created, he was created with a breastplate made of nine gemstones (see Ezek. 28:13-16). If you do a study of these stones, you will find that they match up with the breastplate of the High Priest in the Holy of Holies, all except for three stones (see Exod. 28:17-20). The High Priest's breastplate had twelve stones; three were missing from hillel's (lucifer's) breastplate. The Lord pointed this out to me, and it is interesting that the ones that are missing are lucifer's weak points.

One of the missing stones represents the tribe of Issachar, and Scripture tells us that the sons of Issachar were able to interpret the seasons and the times of the Lord (see 1 Chron. 12:32). History bears this out because when Moses was going to be born, satan had no idea when it would be, and that was why he tried to kill all the babies within a certain number of years. Then satan got wind through the stars and the magi that the king would be born, the Messiah. Again, satan did know when and had Herod kill all the babies in the area of Bethlehem (see Matt. 2:16-18).

Now we come to this generation—satan does not know exactly when Jesus is coming back, but he knows that Israel just became a nation. Now satan figures that the Joshua generation or the Elijah generation or the John the Baptist generation will announce Christ's Second Coming and usher Him in. He recognizes these prophets are probably in the womb now. That was when satan legalized abortion and made you pay for it to get rid of any prophets who might be in the womb. The reason that satan does not know everything is because God purposely left him out because, in God's foreknowledge, He knew that this would all happen.

It is like working on a government project. You are only given a certain part of it, and it is called compartmentalization. You get a classified clearance, but what you are working on does not look like the end objective because you only have a part. That is what God did. He prevented satan from having everything, and that is God's way of having security. The devil does not understand the times and seasons. He cannot interpret them, so he has to reverse engineer the stars, which is how we got astrology. He marked the earth with all kinds of different objects, like pyramids. With these markings, they can measure different seasons and times to try to figure out what God is doing.

EVIL WORKING THROUGH THE FLESH

Now the works of the flesh are manifest, which are these; Adultery, fornication, uncleanness, lasciviousness, idolatry, witchcraft, hatred, variance, emulations, wrath, strife, seditions, heresies, envyings, murders, drunkenness, revellings, and such like: of the which I tell you before, as I have also told you in time past, that they which do such things shall not inherit the kingdom of God.
— GALATIANS 5:19-21 KJV

Witchcraft is the work of the flesh, and it is operating in the psychological realm, even though there is a spirit involved. Evil spirits need to get a witch or a warlock to agree with them, and that is in the flesh, and then they bring it over through authority because human beings are the ones who have the authority. Humans are what the evil spirits are after because humans have greater authority than the evil spirits. All humans, even fallen ones, are legally here on the earth, even if they go to hell because they do not get saved.

Demons know that they can use humans on earth if they can get humans to side with them and their agenda. When someone sides with them and becomes a witch, they start trafficking demons. If Christians are not careful, they can traffic these things even though they are not possessed. All the demons need to do is suggest something that you repeat or cause you to respond a certain way toward someone, which is a work of the flesh and not the spirit.

> *But the fruit of the Spirit is love, joy, peace, long-suffering, gentleness, goodness, faith, meekness, temperance: against such there is no law. And they that are Christ's have crucified the flesh with the affections and lusts. If we live in the Spirit, let us also walk in the Spirit.*
> —GALATIANS 5:22-25 KJV

You have the fruit of the Spirit that Paul laid out for us in Galatians. But you also have the fruit of the *flesh*, and witchcraft is a fruit of the flesh, and it is not a spiritual thing. The demons are disembodied and want a human body to manifest through, so they have to get a human to agree with them. If they cannot get a human to agree, then what they want to say or do goes unsaid and undone because there is no manifestation. They need a body.

Evil spirits can station themselves in places, and you can feel the effects of that, and if you are not careful you might believe that you are feeling those feelings. That is where you get gender confusion and addictions from, but they all started from the outside. You will find out all these kinds of things when you go to

Heaven, but you will not need it then. Do not let the devil tell you or make you think that these are your problems. They are not your problems. Humans were not meant to be confused because we are supposed to be the authority on the Earth.

> *Like a flitting sparrow, like a flying swallow, so a curse without cause shall not alight.*
> —PROVERBS 26:2

God's Word says that an undeserved curse will be powerless to harm you because it can find no place to land. If you go to a witch and sit down in front of them, a familiar spirit will stand beside them, and the witch will ask for an object. They need objects to put curses on you. The familiar spirit is waiting because they have something about you as soon as they get your name. The familiar spirit then goes at the speed of light, which is fast enough to go around the earth eight times in one second, to find any information about you that they can.

I know people who confront devils for a living. In one demonic confrontation, the devil being cast out went to another state, took the letter opener off of the exorcist's desk, and brought it back. The demon put it right before the exorcist, whose office was 1,000 miles away.

The familiar spirit standing next to that witch can tell you your phone number, address, and mother's name, and if this sounds familiar, it is because it happens in Christian services. Derek Prince called a service like this a "Christian séance." The familiar spirit will find out information and relay it to the witch, who will tell you all the details. You are in shock and awe that everything the witch has said is true, and it pulls you into their purposes.

The demon will then decide what he is going to do now that he has your attention. The demon may tell the witch that they see that you will have a car accident in a short time, or in one year someone in your family will die. When you ask, "Who?" The demon asks, "Who is Sally?" "That is my mom!" Now, if you agree with that, your mom dies in a year because you just agreed. The way it works is by demons getting you to agree with them.

You do not want to oppose yourself within yourself because when you do that one part of you is siding with God, and the other soulish part of you is siding with whatever is going on around you. If people like you, you feel good, but you do not feel good when they do not like you. However, neither one should move you, whether you are being worshiped or hated, because they are both wrong.

Jesus was not here to make friends. He was here to make disciples and to buy back humanity. In only three and a half years of ministry, they killed Him. Jesus did not do it for Himself; He did it for the Father. Jesus was sent back for the Father, and He wanted to buy us back, and He did it, but many did not discern their day of visitation (see Luke 19:43-44). Jesus said, "*O Jerusalem, Jerusalem, the one who kills the prophets and stones those who are sent to her! How often I wanted to gather your children together, as a hen gathers her chicks under her wings, but you were not willing!*" (Matt. 23:37). Jesus prophesied this the night before He was betrayed.

Spiritual progress is a process that you go through as you start to move with God. The separation between you and the world happens whether you are actively separating yourself or not. However, you can take that as rejection, which is why you have to discern the things that are happening spiritually. You must discern things that are already coming against you and opposing you. Even though you think everyone likes you, the people of the world cannot like you.

I was in the world, and I worked at a job for 30 years. At work, I witnessed to everyone, and I talked to everyone about the Lord, but I did not go out drinking with them. I did not do the things that they did because I had separated myself. I was not saved until I was 19, but when I was 10, Jesus told me, "You are set apart for ministry, and there are three things I do not want you to do. I do not want you to drink. I do not want you to smoke, and I do not want you to date." Now, I was 10 years old, and I did not get saved until I was 19.

While I was still 10 years old, the Lord took me to Mount Sinai, and I did not know what was going on. I could feel someone standing beside me, and he would protect me, but I did not realize it was an angel until I was saved. On Mount Sinai, the Lord told me that there would be three seven-year sections of my life. He showed me what was going to happen in each one of them. At the end of that time, I would be taken back up to the mountain of God to be with God, and that would be the end of my life and the end of my career. I had not figured it out, but if you add 21 years to my 10 years, it is 31, and I was 31 years old when I went in for that operation, and I died. I went to Heaven, and then I was given an extension. When I came back, my eyes were opened as to how it works in the spirit realm.

I saw that we are being dumbed down by being convinced we are someone we are not. I saw all this confusion among Christians because we are in a war, but no one wants to talk about it. You think that the devil can't touch you as a Christian, right? You believe you have no devil problems because you are in Him, and you practice all of your "in Him" Scriptures. The devil knows those Scriptures, too, but he also knows that you do not understand them. The devil is constantly saying, "Did God say? Does not God know that if you eat of this, you will be like Him?" (see Gen. 3:1-7). However, you already are like Him, and you do not need to eat the fruit.

You constantly feel like you are being left out, but that is a demon because you are in, and they are out trying to get in! The only way they can get in is through you, but if you do not let them in, they cannot. You cannot allow them to gain entrance into your mind and emotions because they will start to control your situations.

ACCOUNTABILITY AND THE FIVEFOLD

You would not believe the people who have come to me in the name of the Lord and prophesied all this doom, and I am still waiting for it. That is not a prophet. The latest thing about a prophet is, it has become prophetic instead of a prophet. The problem now is if you are prophetic, you are not accountable. If you are a prophet, you get stoned, and in the Old Testament, you would lose your life if you were wrong. However, if you are prophetic, well, they are just prophetic, and that is just the way it is. Well, actually, no, it is not.

Did you ever notice that suddenly everyone is apostolic instead of an apostle because then you are not as accountable? Now you can print your certificate out online and be an apostle just like that. Imagine there was an announcement that tomorrow, at three o'clock, everyone who is an apostle must report for beheading. All of a sudden, all those apostles would become evangelists. If you are a true apostle or a true prophet, then you pay the price. Then what happens is you have an authority, and you are part of the governments of God, and it takes years to walk in that.

When people do not pay the price to be an apostle or prophet, what happens is a familiar spirit gets involved. You can be in a service, and it is not the Spirit of God, and I do not know what to say, but it is not God at all or it is in the emotional realm. Familiar spirits will accommodate a person who has not moved on with God. The body of Christ needs true prophets, apostles, pastors, and evangelists, and we need the teachers willing to pay the price. It is not the time to back off right now, and in fact, it is the worst time to do that.

People do not understand that satan does not have any authority over them unless they hand themselves over to an evil spirit. If you do not hand yourself over, these evil entities have nothing to work with you. Now is the time for every Christian to do what God has asked them to do because the body of Christ has got to come into the unity of the faith.

> *And He Himself gave some to be apostles, some prophets, some evangelists, and some pastors and teachers, for the equipping of the saints for the work of ministry, for the edifying of the body of Christ, till we all come to the unity of the faith and of the knowledge of the Son of God, to a perfect man, to the measure of the stature of the fullness of Christ.*
> —EPHESIANS 4:11-13

> *That we should no longer be children, tossed to and fro and carried about with every wind of doctrine, by the trickery of men, in the cunning craftiness of deceitful plotting, but, speaking the truth in love, may grow up in all things into Him who is the head—Christ—from whom the whole body, joined and knit together by what every joint supplies, according to the effective working by which every part does its share, causes growth of the body for the edifying of itself in love.*
> —EPHESIANS 4:14-16

God set in the church the fivefold ministries, not people. God sets it in the church, and then He gives gifts individually as the Spirit wills, not as you will (see 1 Cor. 12:11). We need this because it brings the body of Christ into unity. What you need is every one of these fivefold ministers in your life, and then if you are called to be one of them, you need to be groomed and then fulfill that. We need everyone to fulfill their call because we must come into the unity of the faith, and we cannot accept the false. We have to be able to discern at a higher level to know that something *is* God or it *is not* God.

These evil spirits operate on familiarity, and they study you and know your weak points and how you respond. If you stop responding to their input, they just pass you by, and they find someone weaker. If you want to know a shortcut, the best thing you can do is start laughing because I have found that it is something they cannot handle, and they flip out.

We were just about to leave on our trip to Australia, and I wanted to stop by my office. We had just gotten brand-new tires for our Pathfinder the week before because we were giving to the ministry. We only had to buy two other sets of tires in almost 300,000 miles, which was a miracle. Well, when I came out, the tire was flat. I said, "That's it? That's all you got, devil? You have got to be kidding me! You are at the end of your rope, aren't you?" I went back in, and Kathi called someone to get it fixed while we were away; it was no problem. We got to the airport and spent two weeks in Australia. There are no problems when you start doing things like that.

Remember, these entities used to have bodies when they lived on this earth, but now they are disembodied. They have no expression unless you give it to them, and you let them live through you in some way. They want to experience again what it was like to live in a body, and because of that, they are seeking embodiment all the time. All of these demons used to be in a body, and they understand what it is like to be in one. When they lived on earth, they were in sexual sin, and according to Scripture, that is why the earth was destroyed in the flood (see Gen. 6:1-8).

The world was destroyed because of sexual sin. So you can see what is going on in the earth today, and even in our capital here in the United States. Those in power are draining the swamp and finding out everything that has been going on for years. In reality, it about evil spirits seeking embodiment to control people in power. First, these evil spirits get people bound, and then they can control them, and then they make decisions for you that are wrong. You do not want to oppose yourself within yourself.

In downtown New Orleans, I cannot go down to preach or feed the poor because it is against the law, but the witches can set up all their tables down there. If you have a permit, you can have your table there, but you will not get one because they do not want you evangelizing. You have to have a permit to do anything downtown. I go down there with a group, and the witches have all their tables set up where you can get your palm read and everything. Anything goes with the witches, especially during Mardi Gras, but I am not allowed to preach.

On one occasion, I was with a group of believers. We all spread out, and one by one we began going up to the tables and witnessing to the witches. As we did this, I watched the warlocks stationed everywhere, and they could see this happening. They were looking at me, and they were picking us all out, and the minute they caught what we were doing, they asked us to leave. We walked a block to find a Starbucks, and one of the suspected warlocks we passed on the corner was in the Starbucks waiting for us.

He kept appearing everywhere we went, and this was during the daylight. I had to stop then and ask the Lord, "Why am I here?" He said, "Because I trust you, and this is My city, and I

want it back." Everywhere we go, the Lord says, "This is My country. I want it back." When we were in Geneva, the Lord appeared
to me and said, "I want My city back."

If you are opposing yourself, if you have a war inside of you,
it is hard for you to walk in authority, and you become your own
worst enemy.

> *These things I have spoken to you, that in Me you
> may have peace. In the world you will have trib-
> ulation; but be of good cheer, I have overcome the
> world.*
>
> —JOHN 16:33

You cannot allow the devil to convince you of something that
is not you. You are not a failure, and this is the end of the rope
for the devils that are harassing you. There is not going to be any
more harassment. Many people are supposed to be in full-time,
power-filled ministries, but the devil has been harassing you. It
is time to be launched again. You cannot fail or think of a thing
to doubt or fear right now. Have no doubts that you are in overthrow right now if you will just agree with God!

Chapter 7

TRUE HOLINESS IS OWNERSHIP

Therefore "Come out from among them and be separate, says the Lord. Do not touch what is unclean, and I will receive you. I will be a Father to you, and you shall be My sons and daughters, says the Lord Almighty."
—2 CORINTHIANS 6:17-18

T HE SPIRIT OF the Lord is not happy when we speak against fellow Christians. James talks about the tongue as being a very small member of the body, but it does great things, and like a ship's rudder, it can steer your whole life (see James 3:1-5).

You must be careful with your tongue that you do not curse man, that God has created in His image. You can curse another person just by speaking against them. You do not want to find yourself on the wrong side of the Lord, so be very careful that you do not use your tongue to curse people. God wants us to bless people and let Him be the judge.

James went on to say that your tongue can be lit on fire from the flames of hell (see James 3:6-12). You are made in the image of God. You have to be very careful that what you believe in your heart is right, because when you speak it you could be lit up with the flames of hell.

I think it is interesting that a couple of books did not pass the Councils at first to be accepted into the Bible, and one of them was James. I think the devil may have had something to do with that. If you read the minutes of these Council meetings, at one point they were arguing about how many angels could stand on the head of a pin. They rejected the Book of Jude, and they rejected the Book of James because five criteria caused them not to make the cut at first, but thank God they are in the Bible.

Adam was created in the image of God, and God gave Adam the power to have dominion over the earth (see Gen. 1:26-28). That means that if Adam saw something and he named it, that is what it is still called today. So you go and try to tell a zebra that he is not a zebra. God gave us the power to have dominion over the earth, but then man fell (see Gen. 3:17-24). When Noah got off the ark, God spoke to Noah word for word what He had said to Adam; He told Noah to go, have dominion over everything, and multiply and prosper (see Gen. 9:1-11).

Jesus Christ came and said, *"Whatever things you ask when you pray, believe that you receive them, and you will have them"* (Mark 11:23-24). What you say with your mouth will come to pass, and you shall have it, period. When you pray, you should believe that you have received it, not when you get it, and that is why you must be careful not to speak against the body of Christ.

> *But I say to you that for every idle word men may speak, they will give account of it in the day of judgment. For by your words you will be justified, and by your words you will be condemned.*
> — MATTHEW 12:36-37

You will be held accountable for every idle word that comes out of your mouth. That is also in red and in the New Testament. As I came out of my body and looked at my earthly body on the operating table, I could see the surgeons working on me. Suddenly Jesus said to me, "I said, in Matthew 12:36, you will be held accountable for every idle word that comes out of your mouth." Then He walked right up to me and said, "You know, I meant that." I was thinking, "Whoa, nice to meet You, too, Jesus." You see, I was a talker, and I said anything that came to my mind.

I am from the East Coast, and growing up, people around me said what they wanted to say, and if they had to apologize later, you had to make them apologize. I noticed that when Jesus was with me, everything He said was very calculated because Jesus would get everything that He spoke. Jesus could not joke with me. If I asked Him, "What are You doing today?" If Jesus jokingly answered, "Oh, I was just making another universe." If He said that, it would create one, and that is how I felt around Him. There was a fear, an awesome fear of the power that He had. When I looked into Jesus' eyes, I realized that He could speak things into existence. He had framed the worlds, and He made us in His image so that when we spoke to mountains, they would be removed.

You will start to see a switch where you will start seeing your prayers answered in a short time. Brother Kenneth Hagin taught the people in his church how to pray. On Sunday nights, he would remind people to turn in their prayer requests to the prayer team because they would be meeting Monday morning to pray. He had to start putting out a waiver and say, "Make sure that this is what you want when you turn it in because you are going to get it." They would get everything on the list. Now, that does not go over with everyone's theology. These women could get a hold of God to where Brother Hagin had to tell them to be careful of what they ask for because they would get it.

It is the same thing with your mouth. What if you started getting everything you said? You have to be careful what you say. Can God trust you? A Christian's mouth is not to cut down their own. I am telling you this as a warning because you will start to see things happen in your life in a short amount of time, but you will be eating from the fruit of your lips. Everyone in their heart has been waiting for what is about to hit the earth, but there will be a responsibility with that.

I pray for everyone, and I do not speak against people. Every witch who comes against me, I pray that their eyes are opened.

Every curse that comes at me, I tell it to return to the sender; then you have the witches dying, but I do not want them to die. I want them to repent and be saved. People are dying because they are running off their mouths.

Your world is very small if you are talking against people because there is a whole world out there, seven billion people. I am personally believing for one billion souls, one seventh of the earth, because Jesus told me that I could not lose. I am going to do my thing, and then I am going back with Jesus. However, while I am doing that, I see that so many people are fighting each other.

It is amazing to me that more Christians are coming against the message than the witches. What if you were doing something for God because God had asked you to do it and you cared about people, and as you do it you have Christians coming against you? Do you know how much that hurts? Imagine someone coming back from the dead who does not want to come back, and they get more pushback from Christians, and all they are doing is what God sent them to do.

You have the opportunity that no other generation has ever had, and that is to stand up and shine. Are you ready when you go to prayer to have to hold on tight because the power of God is going to hit you until you are on the floor praying from the power? Are you ready for a firehose? I know you have used your little sprinkler, but are you ready for a firehose?

If you were doing something for God, you would not want your own coming against you. Now, you expect the world to act like monkeys. There are a lot of things from God inside of you, and they have to come out. When they come out, we cannot tolerate Christians stopping Christians from manifesting their gifting and the power of God. I am not going to tolerate it, and I will come against anyone who comes against you. Why? Because we are all part of the same team, and we must turn it around so that the world sees that we are the chosen people of God and will shine in these last days. Our faces are going to shine like the noonday sun. We are going to be wise ones (see Dan. 12:3; Eccles. 8:1).

THE END-TIME CHURCH

I want you to focus on this word: "Now faith is" (see Heb. 11:1). I saw that the church was a type of Enoch in the end times, and I saw that Enoch did not even start walking with God until he was 65 years old, so everyone has a chance. After age 65, Enoch walked with God for 300 years, which will take a lot of faith. Enoch was a prophet, and he did not have anyone with him except God Himself.

Enoch had to go around to all the cities and announce their judgment because they were interbreeding, and there was no repentance for the hybrids. God is a righteous judge, and Enoch went around from city to city, announcing their judgment. Enoch was a prophet, and he walked with God to the point where God found him so irresistible that God took him (see Gen. 5:24). I guarantee you that the days before Enoch disappeared, he was coming in and out, and it was very difficult for him, but he had to do it. *Thus, the church walked with God, and they were not.* God will take the church because it pleased God. That is the way it is going to happen. It should not be that big of a revelation, but obviously it is that the wise ones will shine like the noonday sun in the last days.

If you read all the prophets, it is there, and all the prophets spoke that same kind of language, not just Daniel. They all did, and they all saw at the end of times. Enoch was doing his calling, and he was not in a bomb shelter, eating beans, drinking water, and watching DVDs. Enoch was out proclaiming what the Lord had put in him to proclaim and was proclaiming the pending judgment for the world. Nothing has changed. One of the most profound prophets who ever lived was asked what new good thing God is doing. Had God showed him anything? He said, "Nothing. God is doing the same thing He is always doing."

I am ready to go into a whole other phase myself, and I have already entered into it. There has been so much done, and yet there is so much more to come. We are about to witness the greatest show of God's power that has ever been manifested, but it will come because we are in unity. It is not going to be aborted as a result of not getting it under control. We are going to let God move, but we are going to be smart. We are going to be discerning in these last days. The things that you got away with this year, you are not going to get away with next year. Watch your words, and please do not curse or speak against the body of Christ. Let God be the judge of that.

I have known what I have been called to do since I was ten years old, but there must come a time when you stand up, and you have to defend the faith, and part of defending the faith is coming into unity and finding a way to get along with each other. I received this as a warning from the Lord. Things are about to change because the spiritual atmosphere has shifted, and that means that everything you do now, you do 100 percent for the Lord, full out. You do not hold back because next year, everything will count, as you have never seen before. You watch what happens because it will be a year of *landslide*. It will be a landslide. It will be beyond. You will sow in famine and reap a hundredfold return. I am not going to wait; I am going to start now.

DO NOT BE IGNORANT

Lest Satan should take advantage of us; for we are not ignorant of his devices.

—2 CORINTHIANS 2:11

I asked the Lord to explain some things to me because no one was explaining them, and He opened the spirit realm to me, and I saw our enemy. I held back for some time from speaking about it, but now it is time to start to reveal it to people. The things you are going through are not being resolved. If I do not tell you what is going on around you so that there is resolution, you will always be in the dark, and that is not God's will.

The demons get upset because I am telling all their dirty secrets, and the witches get upset because they lose their power if the demons lose their power. However, the most amazing reaction to me is when Christians have asked me to back off, and it is because of that I am not backing off. Paul said, *"We are not ignorant of his devices."* Now, what does that mean? Why is it that Christians are saying, "I do not know what's going on with me"? Why are they blaming God for things that are the demons' fault? Do I just keep silent?

I asked the Lord to explain to me how you can walk with God, feeling the power and presence of God, and then go out into the world and people seem to suck the life out of you just by being out there. The world is walking in darkness, and if they come near you it gets on you, but what you have does not get on them. The Scriptures show that the High Priest, priests, or Levites could not transfer holiness to another, but if the priest touched something unclean, he had to go through a ritual cleansing (see Lev. 21–22). Yet it says that holiness is not transferable (see Hag. 2:11-14). That means that I cannot transfer holiness to anyone, but they can transfer uncleanness to another according to Scripture. What is holiness, then?

Religion has made holiness about behavior, which is like science because it is based on observation. All of science is observation, from which scientists derive facts. We can observe holiness and make a list of these things that make you holy if you act this way. However, it will be just an observation because true holiness is of the Lord, and it is from another realm; God is holy.

When I finished my study on holiness, I asked the Lord what holiness was, and He told me, "Kevin, holiness is ownership. I buy you out, and I take you into My private stock for my display, and you are Mine. You are set apart." So God bought us and has us on display in this generation, in this dispensation, to display His glory. God is proud, and He is allowed to be proud, and He displays us in this end. Everything that is happening right now is a set up for God to be glorified in the world and this nation.

Everything that is happening in the world right now may be shocking to you, but it is only housecleaning because there is a separation taking place. You should be glad that all this is happening because it shows everyone's true colors, and that is what you want. You do not want to be included in with the world because you will be judged with the world (see 1 Cor. 11:32). You want to stand out and be separate because God owns you, and you are not your own. Your life is not your own.

> *Or do you not know that your body is the temple of the Holy Spirit who is in you, whom you have from God, and you are not your own? For you were bought at a price; therefore glorify God in your body and in your spirit, which are God's.*
> —1 CORINTHIANS 6:19-20

Powerful things happened to me when I realized that my behavior is based on my understanding of who I am in Christ. I started to act like my Father because that is what Jesus did. Jesus said, *"He who believes in Me, the works that I do he will do also; and greater works than these he will do, because I go to My Father"* (John 14:12). Jesus only did what He saw His Father doing. Even when Jesus could have delivered Himself from the cross, He said, *"Not My will, but Yours, be done"* (Luke 22:42). Jesus was able to turn Himself over continually to the Father and be separate. Jesus could have called twelve legions of angels and delivered Himself from the cross, but He did not.

A part of this move of God is the separateness of ownership. God illustrated His purchase of me by handing me a blank check, and He said, "Whatever your price is, I will pay it." He continued, "But in fact, I already have. I bought you out. You are Mine.

You are worth it." God already predetermined that we were all worth it before we were born. Before the worlds were formed, Jesus determined that He was coming back, knowing that man would fall. Why? Because God gave us free will. To make us in the image of God, He had to give us free will.

> *For we are His workmanship, created in Christ Jesus for good works, which God prepared before-hand that we should walk in them.*
> —EPHESIANS 2:10

They had already calculated the risk of giving us free will. It is not talked about, but free will is our greatest asset, and it also could be our greatest liability. Everything is conditional based on what you know and act on; however, you cannot act on it if you do not know. It is very important to gain knowledge and under-standing, and then it is very important to show your faith by what you do. So you have to implement it into the physical realm.

> *And I will give you the keys of the kingdom of heaven, and whatever you bind on earth will be bound in heaven, and whatever you loose on earth will be loosed in heaven.*
> —MATTHEW 16:19

We are His workmanship; we represent Jesus on the earth, and He gave us the power to bind and to loose. Here are two things no one wants to touch. Jesus said, *"If you forgive the sins of any, they are forgiven"* (John 20:23). Jesus also tells us that we can be partakers of the divine nature (see 2 Pet. 1:4). It does not matter what you think because it does not change what God has done for us. However, not knowing about it keeps people in the dark. There is a Chinese proverb, "If you are not rowing, you are part of the problem." Are you a boat anchor, or are you part of the sail?

Huge things are going to start happening in the Spirit. I am talking about angel visitations in your house every night calling you to pray. When Kathi and I traveled, I remember waking up in different countries with an angel in our room. In Israel, every night in the middle of Jerusalem we had an angel in our room. I looked at him, and he said, "You have to pray." I looked at him and said, "We have been all over the world, and I just need a little bit of sleep because we are only getting four hours a night." The angel said, "No one else is available, and God knows that you will do it." So we would get up and pray. You would think that there would be more help, but we all have free will.

We were made in the image of God (see Gen. 1:26). There are no other species like us. There is no one else made in God's image. Jesus came back and died on a cross and bought us back for the Father. Our authority, power, and dominion have been restored to us as children of God. Why do people hide in the darkness at night? Why do criminals work at night? You know, it is one thing to be stolen from and not know it, but it is another thing to let someone steal from you in plain sight. When are we going to stand up and say, "You know what? Not on my watch. I have been assigned to this territory. I have been assigned, and this is my neighborhood, this is my house." When are you going to stand up and say, "There is a new sheriff in town"? We have been given the Word of God to enforce it as judges.

It says in the Bible that Jesus was likened to Melchizedek. It does not say He was Melchizedek because He wasn't. Melchizedek was a person who was the King of Salem and the priest of God Most High. No one confronted him, and no one voted for him, yet he was King of Salem. When Abraham overcame Sodom and Gomorrah and all the kings in the valley, he took all the plunder. Abraham was heading up north into Salem, which is now Jerusalem, and Melchizedek went out to meet him (see Gen. 14:18-20).

Before Moses ever received the Ten Commandments or was on the mountain of fire, Abraham ran into Melchizedek, and he tithed to him before the law was given. Why did Abraham tithe, and how did he know about tithing if the law had not been given yet? Why did Melchizedek bring out the implements of communion before Jesus had His last supper? You still believe in communion, right? Well then, why don't you believe in tithing anymore?

Melchizedek would not let Abraham go through his city with all that unclean plunder. It needed to be set apart. You can take a portion, set it apart to God, and the whole will be set apart. You can take your tongue and set it apart, and the whole will be set apart because it is the rudder (see James 3:4-5). I was in a timeless realm. I did not want to come back because I was limited down here, but I found some things to help people, and I am spending the rest of my life releasing these things.

BE LIKE LITTLE DAVID

If the Spirit of the Lord is where you are, then there is freedom, but if the Spirit of the Lord is not there, there is no freedom. If you go to a church service and the Holy Spirit is not there, get out because there is no freedom there. The Holy Spirit is either in the service, or He is not. If He is not, let's wrap it up and go to Pizza Ranch, but if He is there then let's partake of that table and eat everything on the table. You cannot throw things out just because they do not fit into your little world that is three feet by three feet where me, myself, and I live.

You have to expand out to experience freedom. You have to become a partaker of the divine nature, which means you are trusted to speak those things that are from above (see 2 Pet. 1:4). When you speak, you should speak as though you are speaking the very oracles of God (see 1 Pet. 4:11). The life that we live down here is not our own. There are people all over the world who will not be in church this Sunday because they did not get their way. They will not come to the table.

Did you know that a lot of my spiritual warfare is gone because I have a pastor? Your pastor takes the hits for you. I have been an assistant pastor several times. I was asked to be the head pastor, and I said no because I do not want to be the head honcho. I wanted to be the assistant pastor and make the pastor look good.

The apostles, the prophets, the pastors and teachers and evangelists whom I know do not want to do what they are doing because it is such a great cost. I do not know any prophets who want to be prophets. The prophets I know hide, and they do not want to be known. One prophet I know is the most accurate prophet on the earth, and he has been a pastor for 40 years. He does not want to be known. However, if he gives you a call, you better get ready.

You think you want an angel to come and visit you, but what you forget is they are not just angels; they are *holy* angels. You want the Spirit of God to come into your life in a really strong way, but He is the *Holy* Spirit. You also want to know the Bible, but do you know it is the *Holy* Bible, the Holy Word of God? What does that mean? It means it is set apart, sanctified. It is God's. Abraham walked away with 90 percent; Melchizedek accepted 10 percent. Chapter 13 of Genesis says that Abraham was very rich, but Abraham had left everything to follow God just a few chapters before becoming rich.

I had angels come to me, and I would not recommend it. I'll tell you why. It is because you are accountable for every visitation you have. You are accountable when God speaks to you. If you want God to talk to you, are you ready for the responsibility? I always want to be a mouthpiece for God, but I have to say what He tells me because I have to face God. Do you want to be a prophet? Do you want to be a sent one? Do you want to be an apostle? Do you want to be a pastor?

David was a tremendous king, but what we forget is that he was a warrior. I was taken and shown David when he was at a very young age. He was sitting under a tree, and the livestock were out in the field, and David was picking targets and practicing all day with a slingshot, and he had a harp. We have six strings on our guitar, but David had four on his harp, and he sat there and played all day. Just David and the sheep.

One day when a wild animal came to steal from him, David took it out with his slingshot. He built his confidence up by being in isolation but always practicing, and he got his skill to where he took out a bear and a lion. He worked his way up so that his mindset was already framed in isolation when he was called upon to visit Goliath's battle line (see 1 Sam. 17).

As you know God, David knew God, and he knew how to use what God had given him. When David walked into the battle line scenario, he could not understand why Saul was hiding in his tent, drinking tea, and all his brothers were hiding in their tents, cleaning their armor. In today's terms, it would be like David finding you watching your end-time DVDs, drinking stored up water and eating beans, waiting for the end to come. Little David came in saying, "Wait a minute, what is going on here? Is anybody going to confront this uncircumcised Philistine?"

Uncircumcised means not in the covenant with God. When David said that, it showed that he was relying on the covenant. David said, "How dare you defy the armies of the living God?" He was a boy, but his world was framed in isolation, and God Himself had framed his mindset. David was being groomed for a time that had not yet come. However, on that day, righteous indignation came up within David, and he saw a discrepancy that needed to be corrected, and he rose to the occasion and started asking questions. When David was brought to King Saul's tent, David told the king that he *used* to tend his father's sheep. Why did he say that? Wasn't he still the shepherd? It was because David was about to walk through his door of promotion.

If you could see the angels being stationed worldwide right now and see all the world events that are *not* going to happen, you would understand what is happening in the Spirit. What you are witnessing is history. We throw the name King Cyrus around who helped rebuild the walls, who helped Jerusalem, and he wasn't even a believer. We throw that around, but it is happening again, only it is even better this time. It is time to be like little David, and not be like his brothers, and if you are King Saul, you are about to lose your job.

If you do not discern what is going on around you in your spirit and you take the wrong side of what is happening, you will miss the opportunity that is your promotion. It is not the time to get washed out. I have so many friends who are out of the ministry now because they got washed out. They sat in the same classes I did as Brother Hagin told them not to do this or this or this. They did every one of them, and now they are out of the ministry.

LIFE FROM THE OTHER REALM

When you go to the aquarium, do you look in there and wonder what it would be like to be in that tank with all those fish? The fish are looking at you, thinking, wow, if they could just be out there in your world. You are of a higher order than any other creation, and God gave you everything you have to use for the furtherance of His kingdom. Do not let your tongue be set on fire with the flames of hell. Speak from the altar fire the very words of God for this generation.

Speak out where you are going. I was told to speak where I am going, and I used to say this as a little boy, "I am going somewhere to happen." I would say that all the time, and I did not even know what *happen* was. I did not know what that was, but at least I was talking in that direction. What is coming out of my mouth is life to me. I live off the very words that come out of my mouth because I am talking from the other realm, and it is life. I need just as much help as everyone else does, and I have to do what I am called to do.

When I was in Heaven, I saw that the only way I could affect a generation was to speak from the fire at the altar right there in the front of the throne room. It is a fire that never goes out, and when it touches you, it cures you. It helps you get over the dreaded disease of self.

The first stage that the prophet Isaiah went through was getting caught up and seeing the throne room, and then he was undone (see Isa. 6:1-8). However, the cure was right there at the altar. When that coal touched Isaiah, he was cured, and then he realized he had to go back. So Isaiah asked the Lord to send him. What happened to Isaiah is what has happened to me, but this can happen to everyone, and it is supposed to. Did you know that this is supposed to be a common thing? Enoch just walked over, and he was not because he pleased God (see Gen. 5:24).

I saw when Jesus gazed at me that I was irresistible to Him because He created me. He told me that I turned out just like He thought of me that day. Jesus said, "I remember when I thought of you and breathed you into your mother's womb." He said,

"You turned out exactly how I thought of you," and He was smiling at me.

When I came back, you can imagine how disappointing it was to see the body of Christ not responding and, even worse, withstanding you. When God moves through you, He moves through you for someone else, and He is trying to wrap this up. If it were up to God, He would have already wrapped this up.

I saw something very profound that I have not shared. I saw the nail print in Jesus' hand when He said to me, "We do not have the time we used to have to get people ready for what we have called them to do."

Jesus told me how He had exposed Moses to Egypt for 40 years, and how Moses was educated in the highest of all the universities. Then Moses spent 40 years in the Midian desert because he had to know that desert like the back of his hand. I had never even thought about that. Of course, Moses had to know the desert to take all of God's people through. He knew that place like the back of his hand. Moses had 80 years of preparation to do that.

Jesus told me that in comparison to Moses' years to get ready, we have only days, and He said that time is short. I saw a vision of the white horse. I saw the nail print hand, and it was Jesus' hand steadying that horse. Then I saw the horse was kicking in the stall, ready, and Jesus had His hand out holding the horse by the bridle. I will never forget it because I realized that Jesus is waiting for us to do what He has called us to do. We must become partakers of the divine nature and not back off.

But if I cast out demons with the finger of God,
surely the kingdom of God has come upon you.
—LUKE 11:20

Jesus told me that when He cast out the demon from the demon-possessed man in Luke 11, the Pharisees claimed that He cast out demons by beelzebub, the ruler of demons. Jesus told them that a house divided against itself cannot stand. Then He said, *"But if I cast out demons with the finger of God, surely the kingdom of God has come upon you"* (Luke 11:20).

Jesus said, "Kevin, when I said *with the finger of God,* I was referring to the same finger that they claimed was the finger that wrote the law on the tablets of stone." Jesus said that the Pharisees knew what He was saying. Jesus told them that He was casting out devils by the same finger that wrote their law, and this is the Jesus I met, the One who is the Commander of your faith. Jesus has started your faith and is going to finish it. He is overseeing your life, and He gets what He wants. You have to adhere to this word and know that Jesus has bought you because He wants you, and you are irresistible. You need to come in and let Him put you on display at the end of this age, and let's wrap this up.

Many people feel frustrated right now. Do you think it is because what is in you is the standard for where we are going? Is it possible that what you feel inside is because God placed it there? Did you know that there is treasure inside of you? There are gifts inside of you. People worldwide listen to what has been given to me to say, and their lives are being changed. The whole mindset of Christianity is changing over a flight attendant who prays in tongues.

If God can use a flight attendant and a hairdresser, then what can He do with you? That is why I was sent back. Jesus did not call me apostle or prophet; He called me "Kevin." I am from above, and so are you, and if you diligently sit under your tree and practice with your slingshot, I guarantee you one day you are going to make history. I am not being told to say this except by the Lord Himself.

There are people in Heaven I know, and they are cheering me on. People who were my spiritual fathers when they were alive. People like Brother Hagin, whose every word I adhered to, but now he is sitting up there watching. He just wants someone on this earth to take what he taught for years and do something with it. It is the same as everyone else in Heaven.

There are people in Heaven I talked to who are depending upon us to be faithful now. They laid such a foundation, and they want to meet all of us because we were chosen to be born at the end of this age to wrap it up. We are like the crown molding and all the extra little added things at the end of the age. Everything has been built and framed, but now we are like the ornamentation. Jesus is the author and the finisher of our faith, but we are the finishers of the whole plan of God.

In Heaven, there are the prophets you want to meet, but they want to meet you. Now, I sat and talked to a certain individual in Heaven, and you would know who it was if I named him. I sat and listened to him talk to me for hours of earth time.

He said, "I have been bothering Jesus ever since I got up here because I did not get to finish everything that I wanted to do because my body wore out." He said, "Before I was saved, I abused my body with drugs, and my body did not go as far as my spirit could go. I have been bothering Jesus, and I was so glad when I was told that you are going to take over for me." I said, "Excuse me?" He said, "Well, actually, it is going to take about six of you, but you are one of them. The Lord has instructed me to tell you how to do this." I said, "Okay."

So he sat there and started to tell me step by step the Holy Spirit's operations and the ministry of the evangelist. He explained all of the tactics that he was permitted to share with me. He named the people who were called alongside to help me. Almost every one of those people works for me now. It is not by chance that you find yourself reading this because you are important, but see, it is not by chance that I find myself here also because I am important. The bottom line is that there is a huge plan that has to do with you doing God's heart for a generation, and you will not have anything to worry about if you can hand yourself over.

Chapter 8

LIVING OUT OF YOUR SPIRIT

For as many as are led by the Spirit of God, these are sons of God.

—Romans 8:14

THROUGH JESUS CHRIST, the Father has taken the limitations off of you. Jesus helped me by explaining this to me. He said, "I bought back your spirit by My death and resurrection. I purchased you, but the real you is your spirit man." You have a soul with three parts—your mind, will, and emotions—and tied to that is your organic brain. You also have your emotions tied to the different glands that produce hormones in your body. As a Christian, your spirit man is ignited with God, but your soul is tied to your emotions and the thought processes of your organic brain. All of these parts are housed in your earthly body and tied to it, but remember—inside of you is the real you, your spirit man.

When I died and left my body on the operating table, the real me, my spirit man, was standing beside my earthly body with Jesus. I had on a beautiful robe of righteousness, and I was glowing. I was still me, and nothing had changed except this one thing—I had no limitations anymore. I saw that our spirit has no limitations because we are born again. *"But he who is joined to the Lord is one spirit with Him"* (1 Cor. 6:17).

> *That they all may be one, as You, Father, are in Me, and I in You; that they also may be one in Us, that the world may believe that You sent Me. And the glory which You gave Me I have given them, that they may be one just as We are one.*
> —JOHN 17:21-22

You can see how much Jesus loves the Father in this verse and how much the Father loves Jesus. Jesus is saying that the same love that the Father has for Him the Father has for us. Jesus was talking about the disciples, but He was pointing at us, and He talked about those who will come after. God loves us as much as He loves Jesus and wants us to share in this same unity. They share the oneness that they share with us, and they are one as we are one. This concept seems to fall on deaf ears because many people's minds are not programmed to accept this type of information. Our spirit man is limited because our mind does not always comprehend what it should.

If someone is good enough, they can manipulate you and talk you out of anything. You know what I am talking about because you know that people can manipulate your wallet to where it starts moving in your pocket. They can make you feel like you need something by watching a commercial that is only 33 seconds long. Suddenly you need that, but you don't know why because you did not need it a minute ago. They are using the power of suggestion.

> *Or do you not know that your body is the temple of the Holy Spirit who is in you, whom you have from God, and you are not your own? For you were bought at a price; therefore glorify God in your body and in your spirit, which are God's.*
> —1 CORINTHIANS 6:19-20

My job is to train people to live out of their spirit because, first of all, we are spiritual people. You do not become spiritual just because you pray or read your Bible. You are spiritual because the Spirit of God came in and made you one with Him. He joined with you. Paul told the Corinthians that your body is the temple of the Holy Spirit. You become one in spirit when you join yourself to the Lord.

> *And I, brethren, could not speak to you as to spiritual people but as to carnal, as to babes in Christ. I fed you with milk and not with solid food; for until now you were not able to receive it, and even now you are still not able; for you are still carnal. For where there are envy, strife, and divisions among*

you, are you not carnal and behaving like mere
men?
—1 Corinthians 3:1-3

Paul spoke to the Corinthians, and he called them carnal Christians, but they were still Christians. He said that they were carnal in the sense that they yielded to the flesh. They yielded to their mind, and that was not good, and there was the misuse of the gifts of the Spirit. A lot of things were happening in the church in Corinth that were causing problems. The world was looking at them and saying that they were nuts. Paul said that it was actually reported that there was sexual immorality among them (see 1 Cor. 5:1). Paul recommended that the young man be handed over to satan for the destruction of the flesh so that his spirit may be saved in the day of the Lord Jesus (see 1 Cor. 5:4-5).

You might ask—why? Paul knew that the people of the world are looking at the church, and we have to be different. We have to be set apart and holy. Paul was saying that you need to be spiritual, and you need to live out your spirit. Being spiritual does not mean falling on the ground and praying in tongues and having someone carry you out of a service.

Being spiritual is when you have waited all your life for a situation to happen, and when it does you are tempted to do what you know is wrong, but instead you resist, walk away, and laugh. That is being spiritual because there is no way that you could have walked away, but you did. You have to look down into your spirit because your flesh and your mind will not help you at that moment. It is like you have two against one.

You understand being spiritual when God hits you and you fall under His glory. However, when you are tempted by a woman who is not your wife trying to get into your room, you do not feel very spiritual. She is trying to get in, and you push her out of your room and shut the door. Your body and mind are saying, "Why did you do that?" But your spirit is saying, "I am going to be on Mount Zion among the righteous on the holy sapphire stones forever." You pay the price and deny yourself like we all have to do.

How would you like it if the Lord told you, "I have called you to be part of the fivefold ministry of the church. I do not want you to go into the Air Force Academy. I do not want you to be an F-16 pilot. I want you to go to college where you will learn My Word. After many years I will put you in the ministry."

I had 21 years of training, and then I had another 30 years at a company where I did not even want to be. You think you are a prophet, but you might be a non-prophet. You might not be prophetic. You might be pathetic. Until one day, God sees in you that jewel, and He is going to work it out to where you *will* operate in what you are called to do, and that is so key.

Years later, I was presented three different times with the opportunity to go back into the Air Force and fly F-16 fighter jets. One of them was for the state of Oklahoma as an Air National Guard. I would not have to go into the Air Force, but I could go into training, and then I would get an F-16 fighter jet. Opportunities like this happened three different times, and each time it happened I would fast and pray even though I knew what the Lord was going to tell me.

I figured I could twist God's arm by fasting and praying, "Lord, can I please have this?" It was all set up because I knew the commanders. I knew everyone. I even got invited to do training as a courtesy from the Air Force. It was a complimentary ground school, but then I got to go in the simulator, and I did so well they said they could sign me up. I had to say no because you have to walk away from some things to be in the will of God. You might not think that I know what you are going through, but I do. Only I never forget who took me to the dance because I have that ride home. You get to dance with the One who brought you, and that is Jesus.

I am not all that, and I am never going to be all that, but Jesus is. I will never be, as long as I keep that perspective. I have had people way above me call me, and they all tell me, "Please do not change. Please stay humble." They said, "We have seen people go to nothing when they get to where you're at, and you keep staying who you are, please continue to stay humble." I said, "Fine with me, because God reminds me every day, and so does my wife. I am not all that."

IN YOU AND WITH YOU ALWAYS

Therefore, if anyone is in Christ, he is a new creation; old things have passed away; behold, all things have become new.
—2 CORINTHIANS 5:17

Your spirit is ignited and knows no defeat, and you are going to find this out, and you will say, "Kevin was right." Your spirit is as holy and as righteous as it is ever going to be. The real you inside is born again of the Spirit. If you are a new creature in Christ, then old things have passed away. There is nothing old about you now; everything is new. If you are a Christian, you must believe that. You no longer know any defeat. The Spirit of God has never been defeated, and the Spirit of God has never thought that He was going to fail, and He has never had a bad thought. The Spirit of God is inside of you, married to your spirit.

> *Where can I go from Your Spirit? Or where can I flee from Your presence? If I ascend into heaven, You are there; if I make my bed in hell, behold, You are there. If I take the wings of the morning, and dwell in the uttermost parts of the sea, even there Your hand shall lead me, and Your right hand shall hold me.*
>
> —PSALM 139:7-10

That is why the psalmist said, "Wherever I go, You are there." You are part of Him, and He is part of you. As a spiritual person, you may have often been told that you do not have any fun. You are told that you can't do any of this, or you can't do any of that. However, if you want to participate in the supernatural and want everything fixed in your life, you will have to yield to your spirit because that is where the Spirit of God is. The Spirit of God is not going to lead you in the wrong way.

> *For those who live according to the flesh set their minds on the things of the flesh, but those who live according to the Spirit, the things of the Spirit. For to be carnally minded is death, but to be spiritually*

*minded is life and peace. Because the carnal mind is
enmity against God; for it is not subject to the law
of God, nor indeed can be. So then, those who are in
the flesh cannot please God.*
—ROMANS 8:5-8

If you were a carnal Christian (and good luck with that!), you
would encounter a whole list of things in this life that do not
match up with what is in your book in Heaven. You will be in
the permissive will of God instead of the perfect will of God.
You are going to have a lot of cuts and bruises until you come
to the place where you realize that being spiritual can be fun
because it is rewarding, and you are sowing into your future. You
are sowing into what God has for this generation because it's not
just about you. It is about everyone around you.

*For if you live according to the flesh you will die;
but if by the Spirit you put to death the deeds of the
body, you will live.*
—ROMANS 8:13

In Corinth, Paul had to hand one of the carnal Christians
over to satan for the destruction of his flesh because he yielded to
the flesh. Anyone who walks according to the flesh is an enemy
of God because the flesh wars against the Spirit. Those who walk
in the Spirit are called sons of God (see Rom. 8:14). It is satanic
for anyone to make you think, as a spiritual person, that you are
one of those weird people who will not have any fun. I still have
fun, but I have fun within the boundaries of safety. I do not have
to be carnal and yield to the flesh, which is death. The flesh is

selfish, and the flesh is what is limiting you. If you take the limitations off of your life, it will be because you yield to the Spirit of God.

> *I was with you in weakness, in fear, and in much trembling. And my speech and my preaching were not with persuasive words of human wisdom, but in demonstration of the Spirit and of power, that your faith should not be in the wisdom of men but in the power of God.*
> —1 CORINTHIANS 2:3-5

Paul spoke spiritual things out of his spirit. If you begin First Corinthians 2 and read down to verse 10, Paul begins to talk about how God reveals the deep things to us through His Spirit. We have received not the spirit of the world but the Spirit who is from God that we might know things freely given to us by God. But a carnal man does not understand spiritual things, for they are spiritually discerned. As a Christian, you are spiritual, and whether you like it or not, you do not have to be spiritual; *you are spiritual.* So you can stop trying *to be* because *you are.* You are all that.

You are spiritual because you can choose to sow toward the Spirit, and you have a choice to listen to your spirit, which is down inside of you. Your mind will take what your spirit is saying and analyze it according to what is up there. If you only have the world's education up there in your mind, that could be a problem. I can use my mind to fly a jet because I put the information up there. If you switched me over to another jet, I could study and learn to fly that jet. You would not be able to fly a jet if you never studied and put that information into your mind.

PROTECTING YOUR INFLUENCE

What I am talking about is the transformation of your mind that comes by the Word of God (see Rom. 12:2). Your soul, which is your mind, will, and emotions, is another entity that will not automatically side with your spirit. Carnal Christians are Christians who are trapped in their body and their thinking, and their spirit is in a prison.

What happens is that demons understand domains, and they understand the territories of influence that they have. The enemy wants to separate you and partition you out to where demons can get in there and dwell in those areas within. I am not talking about being possessed. I am talking about demons having a stronghold within you. In a country where the Gospel is being preached regularly, most people are brought up with an element of God in their life. In that case, it is hard for a demon to get full control of a person.

In countries where their religion, military, and government are all wrapped up in one, you will have many possessions. When you join the military in these countries, their religion *is* part of the military. Most governments have an element of religion within them, and the element of religion in most militaries is usually hidden. However, there is full hatred of Christians and Jews in some countries, and it is not hidden at all. These countries build their whole mindset around that hatred.

Just as religion has gotten into the military, it can be the same thing with you. You have to be careful that you do not allow yourself to be partitioned out to where there are domains available to be occupied by the enemy. If you release a certain area of yourself to the flesh and carnal nature, then you have partitioned it out for a demon spirit to come in and influence you in that area. That is not possession, but it is influence.

Carnal Christians can be like a submarine that has screen doors. You do not want a screen door on a submarine; you want it sealed up. As a Christian, you have got to be sealed up. The demons understand dominion and domain. The Greek word for demon possession is *demonized*, and it is not demon-possessed like you think. It has to do with proximity. It is all about influence and how much of yourself you have handed over to the devil. The question is not if you have a devil or not. It is how much have you yielded yourself to the devil?

You must understand that you have full authority over yourself, and if you give the demons permission, they will come right in. As Christians, they are not allowed to come past a certain point, but they will never stop trying to access partitions within you. That is why it is so important that you are a born-again, Spirit-filled Christian who prays in tongues to build your spirit up. You must also fortify your mind with the truth in the Word of God.

Paul was more about false doctrine than you may want to believe. You can see in the Bible how much Paul was trying to protect the Christian faith from false doctrine. He was so much more than a preacher or teacher of the faith. Paul was a protector and father of the faith. Paul said, *"For though you might have ten thousand instructors in Christ, yet you do not have many fathers; for in Christ Jesus I have begotten you through the gospel. Therefore I urge you, imitate me"* (1 Cor. 4:15-16).

The war that is going on inside of you can be put to nothing by getting your soul to side with your spirit and then ganging up on your body to obey. Paul said it this way, *"I discipline my body and bring it into subjection,"* which in Greek means he beat it black and blue. He continued and said, *"Lest, when I have preached to others, I myself should become disqualified"* (1 Cor. 9:27). In other words, he did not go out and yield to the flesh in order to protect himself from becoming disqualified.

Paul told the church in Corinth that he wanted to come to them the year before, but that satan stopped him (see 1 Thess. 2:18). Can you imagine Paul the apostle being stopped? What about Jesus when He went to His hometown? He could not heal anyone except a few sick folks with minor ailments because of their unbelief. The Son of God was hindered as a son of man because of people's unbelief. Jesus could not do many miracles there (see Matt. 13:58; Mark 6:5).

> *So then faith comes by hearing, and hearing by the word of God.*
> — ROMANS 10:17

All of this has to do with warfare, and you have to know where your limits are, and your limits are in your faith and others' faith. You can build your faith up, but if you have not produced faith in others, they will not receive. You can be right and walk away like Jesus shaking His head because they saw Jesus as a carpenter's son. They did not see Him as the son of David, the Messiah.

Your spirit is lit up with the power of God right now. In the age to come, you will stand on Mount Zion with all the spirits of the just men made perfect on the fiery stones. When you are standing there in the age to come, you will look back in your spirit and see nothing different now than what you are experiencing on Mount Zion. There was nothing different. I saw that deep within me was this person who could not fail because Jesus had married me, and I was one with Him in Spirit.

You will see that it was your body and mind that were lying to you on earth. People you thought were your friends would come and lie to you and mistreat you and do terrible things to you. You were doing everything you could do to follow Christ, and they were calling you telling you stuff, and they were writing and e-mailing you. They would tell you terrible things, and they were trashing you. All this happened because their partitions got broken into, and evil spirits started to work themselves into those people. You will have to choose who you can be around now.

You have been doing everything right because you sealed everything up within yourself. You have pushed the demon spirits out of your territories that you are taking back. You are taking more and more territory every day. As you do this, your influence will begin to increase to the point where the demons start to leave the building before you get there. The demons know they will get beat up, and they do not want to hear what you will say because it is a judgment to them.

All of this is fine, but you will have to deal with your friends and family next. Those spirits will go out and try to find people you know with a weak link in them and get into them. The demons start to talk to their minds, and suddenly they will get so mad at you over nothing. They will give you a call and trash you, and you are thinking, "What in the world just happened?" When those evil spirits could not get to you, they went out to find a weak vessel.

If they cannot find someone in your family because you shut that down, then they will find random people to harass you. It might be someone who is a total stranger who comes up to you at an airport and starts trashing you. The minute I get off the plane, the evil spirits assigned to that city are waiting for me through someone. I watch the demon enter the person as they are coming down the aisle. I have to have people around me so that they do not try to knock me over or run into me and grab my bags before I can get them off the turnstile. It is because I have satan on the run, and he is leaving town.

Sometimes when you have finally driven the devil out of your house, he puts up his little pup tent in your yard. You have got to go out there and just pull those tent pegs up and say. "I said, leave the city!" Then that evil spirit leaves the city, and your relative from another state calls you and trashes you. It is the same spirit. However, it is all about dominion. When you finally drive satan out of your domain altogether, he cannot fool with you anymore.

You see, in your spirit is where you have dominance, and it is where you have to stay as a Christian. Christians need to know how to live every day and not just get a drive-by on weekends. If I do not cause them to walk like I am walking, then I have failed. Jesus' whole goal was to get His disciples to walk like He was so He could leave. Toward the end of Jesus' three and a half years of ministry, when the disciples could not cast the devil out, or the person did not get healed, He would say, "How long will I be with you" (see Matt. 17:17). Jesus knew that His time was getting short, and He needed that transference to happen.

It is the same with you because you have to walk in this. I am not hiding anything from you because I do not have that kind of authority and power. Only God can hide things. If I am supposed to tell you something, then I need to tell you even if it makes you better than me. Even if it is to the place where you do not need me anymore, and I have worked myself out of a job. I do not have to hold on to the ministry that tightly to where I always have to keep it so that you need me. If I just told you everything and you didn't need me, I would be so happy because I could just stay home.

PUT ON GOD'S YOKE

Jesus' goal was to replicate Himself, and He told us that we were going to do even greater things than He did (see John 14:12). What minister would say that? Jesus did, and He set a precedent. Do not look at people like, "That is a man of God! That is a woman of God!" Maybe they were just obedient and put the yoke of God on them and learned of Him, as Jesus said (see Matt. 11:29-30). What if you are supposed to put the yoke of God on too? What if you put the flesh under and transform your mind by renewing it by the Word of God and letting the Holy Spirit live through you, through your flesh and your mind and your spirit?

Jesus told me that there were no limitations placed on me. That was all new to me because all I have ever been told my whole life was everything I would never be able to do. Why would my parents tell me I was never going to amount to anything? What parent would say that? That was a devil. When I would tell them that the Lord loves them, He has a plan for their life, and the Bible is full of promises, my dad would say, "Don't bring the Bible into it." I was dealing with evil spirits because no parent would be that way. You have to live out of your spirit to discern that what is being told to you is correct.

> *God is Spirit, and those who worship Him must worship in spirit and truth.*
> —JOHN 4:24

You have to discern the *origin* of what is being spoken, and not just what is being spoken. I was shocked at how many people do not speak from their spirit. That is where the Spirit of God is. The Spirit of God is not in your head because God is not a mind, and He is not a body. God is a Spirit, and those who worship Him must worship Him in Spirit and truth. God has a spiritual body, and He has a spiritual mind, and He *does not* have a carnal mind and *does not* have a carnal body. God made us in His image in our spirit, and we have to develop that in our minds and bodies. When this occurs, you will not need me anymore.

You will need a pastor. I have been offered a pastor position in one of the biggest churches. I told them that I am not called to be a pastor. Not that long ago, I was offered a pilot's position with my favorite jet. I told them I am not called to be their pilot. I am living out of my spirit, and if you choose to walk in the Spirit, things will happen really fast inside of you. You will know what just happened in the Spirit, and you will wonder why no one is responding. You know that healing is in the room, and others miss their opportunity by not living out of their spirit.

I have never given a prophetic word to make someone feel good or because I wanted to. I have only given a word after making sure that it was from my spirit and the Spirit of God. I speak it because the Holy Spirit moves me, but many people did not even write it down or even remember it. When it happens, I watch them testify, sometimes on TV, and they never mention that it was spoken to them because they forgot. That is not the way to live.

> *This charge I commit to you, son Timothy, according to the prophecies previously made concerning you, that by them you may wage the good warfare, having faith and a good conscience, which some having rejected, concerning the faith have suffered shipwreck.*
> —1 TIMOTHY 1:18-19

Paul is saying here that you are supposed to wage war with the prophecies you receive. You might ask why you would have to wage war with them if God spoke them through the prophets. Won't it happen if God wants it to happen? No, no, no. Why then would Paul have said to use your prophecies as weapons of war? It is by faith that you receive them because we are in the New Testament, and we walk by faith.

He who dwells in the secret place of the Most High shall abide under the shadow of the Almighty. I will say of the Lord, "He is my refuge and my fortress; my God, in Him I will trust."
—Psalm 91:1-2

The devil cannot operate with you when you are living out of your spirit. You are beyond a challenge to him, and he will not even approach you if you are in the spirit because he cannot. No demon will come near you when you are in the secret place. A demon cannot beat you in the ring with God, but he can beat you in his own ring. The demons do not play by the rules, and all they want to do is get you into their boxing ring where they have a chance of defeating you.

Because you have made the Lord, who is my refuge, even the Most High, your dwelling place, no evil shall befall you, nor shall any plague come near your dwelling; for He shall give His angels charge over you, to keep you in all your ways. In their hands they shall bear you up, lest you dash your foot against a stone.
—Psalm 91:9-12

That is why satan tries to draw you out away from the Spirit. If you are in the Spirit, in the secret place, no evil can befall you (see Ps. 91:10-12). You will not even trip on a stone because the angels will be there to pick you up. It says no disease—nothing will touch you. People get into accidents and die before their time because they have not stayed in the secret place.

You shall tread upon the lion and the cobra, the young lion and the serpent you shall trample underfoot. "Because he has set his love upon Me, therefore I will deliver him; I will set him on high, because he has known My name. He shall call upon Me, and I will answer him; I will be with him in trouble; I will deliver him and honor him. With long life I will satisfy him, and show him My salvation."

—Psalm 91:13-16

I would rather believe the Word of God because God is not a liar. He is not a man that He can lie (see Num. 23:19). God is always going to tell the truth, and the truth is in Psalm 91:9-16. However, to activate it you must first do what is written in Psalm 91:1-2. You must dwell in the secret place of the Most High and abide under His shadow. You must make the Most High your dwelling place. *Then* all of these things will happen.

Chapter 9

THE BLOOD WAS ENOUGH

By that will we have been sanctified through the offering of the body of Jesus Christ once for all.
—Hebrews 10:10

THE LIMITS CAN be taken off immediately by invoking the blood covenant of Jesus. Immediately! It is representing something that God did for us. God bought something for us. What was it? You have to know what it is. The demons know. The demons were after the bloodline because they knew if they did not get to the bloodline of the Messiah, He would be a pure, unblemished Lamb who was slain. Jesus' sacrifice would go through and be accepted, and we would be redeemed. If satan could get hybrid blood into the bodies of all the generations, then when Mary had Jesus it would be a blemished lamb, and the bloodline would be tainted.

> *Knowing that you were not redeemed with corrupt-*
> *ible things, like silver or gold, from your aimless*
> *conduct received by tradition from your fathers, but*
> *with the precious blood of Christ, as of a lamb with-*
> *out blemish and without spot.*
>
> —1 PETER 1:18-19

When men began to multiply on the earth, they began to interbreed between species (see Gen. 6:1-8). The Lord saw that the wickedness of man was great and was sorry that He had made man on the earth. Only Noah found grace in the eyes of the Lord. Noah was the only one in his family who was perfect. He was a just man, perfect in his generations, and he walked with God (see Gen. 6:9). He was perfect in his genetics, and he had not interbred. Noah and his family were the only ones who qualified for the ark. On the other side of the flood, they repopulated the earth. Jesus said, *"But as the days of Noah were, so also will the coming of the Son of Man be"* (Matt. 24:37).

> *For the life of the flesh is in the blood, and I have*
> *given it to you upon the altar to make atonement for*
> *your souls; for it is the blood that makes atonement*
> *for the soul.*
>
> —LEVITICUS 17:11

The blood was so important because the life was in the blood. The blood needed for the sacrifices in the temple had to be perfect. When the people came to sacrifice at the temple in Jerusalem, their sacrifice had to be inspected by the religious system, the Pharisees, and the priests. People from all over the world would come and offer their sacrifices, but the Pharisees and priests would reject some and say that they were blemished. Then they would sell the family a replacement sacrifice, which they had rejected from a previous person's sacrifice. That was called money changing, and it was unfair. That was why Jesus went to the temple and flipped over all the money changers' tables (see Matt. 21:12-13).

All the generations are listed in the Bible because it shows that each person had not interbred with the fallen ones. The enemy was hoping to be able to go to God and say, "I got You because right here, I was able to get into the bloodline." Jesus was the perfect Lamb of God, and that is why the blood is so powerful.

The blood has a voice. When Cain killed Abel, God said, *"What have you done? The voice of your brother's blood cries out to Me from the ground"* (Gen. 4:10). So blood has a voice. The blood of Jesus Christ is speaking, and the blood is so important. The demons react to it the way they do because you are acknowledging that the sacrifice was accepted. Jesus' blood is what has defeated their whole plan. I saw this in Heaven and I came back to get people to see that the sacrifice was accepted. The demons want to get people off that point somehow.

I have read a book that tells you that if you want your church to grow, do not talk about the blood anymore because that is offensive, and take the crosses out of your church. The author gives you ten things you can do to grow your church and not offend people. It is a bestselling book by an author you would know. Once they took the blood of Jesus and the cross out of the church, I do not think that Jesus would be there either.

> *For we do not wrestle against flesh and blood, but against principalities, against powers, against rulers of the darkness of this age, against spiritual hosts of wickedness in the heavenly places.*
>
> —Ephesians 6:12

I saw that when I mentioned the blood of Jesus, the demons got really uncomfortable to the point where they were flipping out. I heard them say. "Don't talk about the blood. It is very dangerous." I asked, "Why?" I heard this one demon scream out as he came flying by me, and he said, "Because it has defeated us!" The demon's blood was imperfect through interbreeding, and therefore irredeemable, and the flood extinguished them.

Jesus told me that they knew everything that was going to happen. He said, "When I play chess, I always win. No one will ever get Me in checkmate because I always reserve the last move for Myself." He said, "I make the board and the game pieces, and I always win."

> *For the weapons of our warfare are not carnal but mighty in God for pulling down strongholds, casting down arguments and every high thing that exalts itself against the knowledge of God, bringing every thought into captivity to the obedience of Christ.*
>
> —2 Corinthians 10:4-5

Demons are beings that have lost the ability to be redeemed. They are going to hell, and they are really upset about it. That is what you are dealing with, and there is nothing that anybody can do about it. They cannot be redeemed. They seek embodiment to get back into a body to express themselves to destroy God's creation. You cannot let them in. As Christians, you cannot let anything that exalts itself above the knowledge of God rule you. You must bring every thought into captivity to the obedience of Christ, and that is spiritual warfare.

The weapons of your warfare are not carnal, but they are mighty through God for pulling down strongholds. Praise God! Then Paul says to bring into captivity every thought, but that means in your mind. These entities cannot do a thing unless they get inside your mind and gain expression through you. It starts in your mind, and if you stop it from manifesting, nothing can happen. Christians go through things like this in their mind all the time, and they do not want to talk to me or anybody else about it. Welcome to spiritual warfare. These spiritual entities need to overthrow you. You have to give them permission, or they cannot get in.

When someone walks up to you and is mad at you and says something bad, start laughing because you will find out real quick who is behind it. If someone is really mad at you, mention the blood of Jesus, and you will suddenly find out that they have invisible friends that are mad at you, and it will split it apart. You will suddenly wonder who you are talking to because they are a woman who now has a man's voice. When demons encountered Jesus, they knew who He was. They cried out, *"You are the Christ, the Son of God!"* (Luke 4:41). Jesus rebuked them and did not allow them to speak. Are you excited that this is what is going to happen with you?

AUTHORITY WHEREVER YOU GO

Jesus was told to cross over to the other side, and He asked His disciples to go with Him in the boat (see Mark 4:35-41). Jesus did not do anything unless His Father told Him to, and He did not say that they were going to sink halfway across. He said, "Let us cross over to the other side," and then Jesus got out His pillow and went to sleep.

Halfway across, a huge windstorm came out of nowhere. It was the territorial spirit, the legion that was in the demon-possessed man on the other side. He was already going to stop Jesus because he knew what was about to happen. The waves were beating into the boat, and the disciples woke Jesus up and asked, "Teacher, don't You care that we are perishing?" Jesus arose and rebuked the wind, and because He addressed the devil it stopped immediately.

When they got to the other side, as soon as Jesus stepped His foot on the shore, that demon-possessed man came down and started confronting Him (see Mark 5:1-17). The demons knew they were on their way out and started to negotiate with Jesus and begged Him not to torment them before their time and not send them out of the area. There was a herd of swine nearby, and all the demons begged Jesus to cast them into the swine. At once, Jesus permitted them. When the unclean spirits entered the pigs, the herd ran violently down the steep embankment and into the sea, and they all drowned.

Why would Jesus do that? There was a temple of Zeus just above that area where they kept the herd of pigs to make sacrifices out of them. Jesus took care of that, as well as the pigs. Everyone in the city came out to find 2,000 pigs drowned and the demon-possessed man sitting clothed and in his right mind, and they were afraid. Then they pleaded with Jesus to depart from their region. Jesus got back in the boat with the disciples and went back across. Think about it—Jesus went the whole way over there, almost got killed, cast the devil out, got back in the boat, and went back across. It was a setup. God wanted to pick a fight.

Samson's mother had an angel visitation before he was born (see Judg. 13:1-5). The angel told her that she would have a son who was anointed of the Lord. She was told not to touch wine and not let Samson touch wine, and that a razor was never to come upon his head. Samson was to be a Nazirite to God from the womb, and he would begin to deliver Israel out of the Philistines' hands.

God did all this because He sought a reason to incite war with the Philistines. That was why Samson was born. He was born to pick a fight. The anointing would come upon him, and all Samson would do is start a war. Jesus, when He comes, starts a war, and everywhere He goes a war starts. In Jesus' day, it was the Pharisees confronting Him. The religious ideas interwoven into your personality's fabric are what you must go after even within yourself. It is not okay to be in debt. You know you have problems, but you think that God loves you and He understands. Yes, but God wants transformation, and He wants you to be a sign and a wonder in your generation.

I worked for a company for 30 years. When I witnessed to people, they would say, "Well, what do you have that I don't have? I have the same job, and I'm making the same amount of money that you are. What more do you have?" I would say, "What I know about *you* is there is a wonderful book written about you in Heaven, and when you become born again, that book is opened." They would look at me and say, "I want that!" They would get saved just off of knowing that.

The crux of my ministry is Psalm 139:16. Each one of your days was written in a book before one of them came to pass. God saw your unformed body being formed in your mother's womb. People know what you believe by how you act. If the people in the world know what you believe, they will not touch you, and they will listen to you. I have seen so many flight attendants and pilots start breaking down and crying when I talk to them about how good God is. It has led many of them to repentance, and they gave their lives to the Lord because I talked about their books. I talked about this wonderful God who wrote books. It is a romantic story of how God loves us, and He writes about us and He forms us in our mother's womb.

FALL BACK ON THE BLOOD COVENANT

And they overcame him by the blood of the Lamb and by the word of their testimony, and they did not love their lives to the death.

—REVELATION 12:11

Make yourself available to God. Turn yourself over to Him and invoke the blood; then the covenant steps in, and the demons cannot go any further. When you acknowledge the blood, it is a border, and it represents a covenant that cannot be revoked.

God has promised that the blessings of Abraham are ours. The curse has been broken.

Christ has redeemed us from the curse of the law, having become a curse for us (for it is written, "Cursed is everyone who hangs on a tree"), that the blessing of Abraham might come upon the Gentiles in Christ Jesus, that we might receive the promise of the Spirit through faith.

—GALATIANS 3:13-14

You have to believe that we are now the children of Abraham. What was the faith of Abraham? He saw Him who was invisible. He was searching for a city whose builder and maker was God. Abraham longed to see these days, and he did not see them, but he was forward-looking. It says their faith did not see the end because they did not get to see Jesus, but they spoke and they built a foundation, all those prophets, everyone listed in Hebrews 11. It says that they did not obtain the promise.

What was the promise? Jesus Christ, the Messiah. That was the end of their faith, not money or anything they were believing for; it is not talking about that. Do you see how we can mix that up? It is talking about the patriarchs of our faith who were in their generation doing their jobs so that you would not have to work as hard. We can grow in the Lord because so many other fathers of the faith have paved the way before us.

What is it about someone who is really a father in the Lord? They want you to exceed them. Did Jesus not want us to exceed Him? Does that sound sacrilegious? Think about it, because there are people who say you cannot be better than Jesus. Jesus said, *"Most assuredly, I say to you, he who believes in Me, the works that I do he will do also; and greater works than these he will do, because I go to My Father"* (John 14:12).

Well, have you walked on water yet? We better start practicing. Everything that Jesus did, you are going to do. No matter what translation you read, it does not explain it away. And you are going to do even greater works than these. Some people try to explain that away; they are the same people who say the Red Sea was only a foot deep when the Israelites walked across. That would only make it a bigger miracle because then Pharaoh's whole army drowned in only a foot of water. This thought was not originally mine, but it rings true.

> *Grace and peace be multiplied to you in the knowledge of God and of Jesus our Lord, as His divine power has given to us all things that pertain to life and godliness, through the knowledge of Him who called us by glory and virtue, by which have been given to us exceedingly great and precious promises, that through these you may be partakers of the divine nature, having escaped the corruption that is in the world through lust.*
> —2 Peter 1:2-4

The blood of Jesus speaks, and it is a border that has been made, and the devil knows that border, but do you know that border? The covenant that was cut is based on exceedingly great and precious promises. These precious promises have been given to us so that we can be partakers of the divine nature through these promises. I fall back on the Covenant. Many generals of the faith and those whom I have talked to all say, "I fall back on the covenant constantly."

My mind started to change around the fact that if God has adopted me, then He has taken responsibility for me. I am going to be a good son, and God is not going to be mocked. Whatever Word of God I have, I will sow it into my life so that it is there when I need healing. Whatever I need help in, it is there because the Word of God is there. Unfortunately, these devils know more about the blood than we do, and that should not be.

The demons understand how they were defeated and disembodied, but they are still roaming the earth, and they are territorial. Wherever you go, you encounter them. I encounter them every time I get off an airplane. People will start to manifest in whatever territory I am, and they just come up and start confronting me. They do not want me in their city. It is a territorial thing, and it's real, but I am not afraid of it. That is why you have got to say, "You know what, devil, you are not touching my children. You are not touching my family. Don't even look at my car, and don't even look at my job."

When I make an album, it goes through a huge process by masters and mixers who are Spirit-filled people who pray in tongues. They are all very good at what they do. They know not to take out every mistake because I want to capture the environment that it was recorded in, but I also want to make sure that everything is right. The person mixing the last album was staying up all night to get it done on time. The night before she was supposed to be finished, she woke up to a giant spirit over her saying, "Don't finish that album." It was threatening her not to finish the album. The demon never came to me.

A separate person masters the album. Just before the woman who mixed it was about to send it to the guy to master it in another state, he called her. He told her that it must be time for Kevin Zadai to put out another album because he just had a demon-possessed man come into his studio. She said, "You're right, and it will be there in 24 hours." She said the last time they put out my album, which made the Billboard charts, his whole system shut down.

You may not even like this type of music, but it is not about the music. It is about what is *behind* the music. We are still getting reports from the first album that came out three years ago. People are continuing to get rid of demons and getting healed while listening to it. One lady just got her right eye healed while listening to it, and demons are leaving people. That is after three years of it being out there.

The blood of Jesus does this. The blood of Jesus speaks—it is a tone, a sound, a smell, and it is dimensional. It is a life, and it is sacred and holy, and no demon can dispute its effect. It is already complete. The blood represents a covenant where God spoke concerning you, and if you relied on that covenant, a lot of your problems would disappear.

The blood is not by merit because it has already been done, and it is very powerful. It speaks more powerfully than you could ever speak, but you have to invoke the blood so that the demons honor the border. You must also invoke the blood because it is falling back on the covenant. The covenant is that *"The Lord will make you the head and not the tail; you shall be above only, and not be beneath, if you heed the commandments of the Lord your God, which I command you today, and are careful to observe them"* (Deut. 28:13).

> *There should be no poor among you, for the Lord your God will greatly bless you in the land he is giving you as a special possession.*
> —DEUTERONOMY 15:4 NLT

God said that many nations will come to you and submit to you, but you will not submit to any, and you will rule over many (see Deut. 28). He said that they will fear you in all the nations around you, and you will lend to many nations, but you will not borrow from any. That was the Old Testament covenant. Paul said that the New Testament is based on better promises, a better covenant.

I saw that prosperity had to do more with authority than it had to do with giving, and it had to do with dominion. Do you think that I will have to pull and twist God's arm to give me something because I give Him something? Do you think that if I ask God five hundred and one times for something that He will get so tired of hearing it, He will give it to me to shut me up? Many people have been indoctrinated with this mentality.

Many people's prosperity is being held up because of demonic spirits because the covenant is already speaking. You have been spoken for, and you are the blessed of the Lord. I was blessed when I had no money, and I am blessed when I do have money. I have learned to live with both, as Paul said (see Phil. 4:12-13). Now I am a distribution center because when I did not have it and then got it, I realized it is not mine.

The blood of Jesus establishes borders. It also establishes a backstop for you for the covenant. You fall on the covenant. Every morning, I wake up, and I tell the Lord, "I'm not all that, Lord, and if You don't help me today, it is going to be bad." I tell Him every day, "I need Your help. I am not leaving this house unless You get in the car with me." I cannot do anything without Him (see John 15:5). When was the last time you have heard that? You hear people say, "Just do it," right before they fall into a big smoking hole, and they are yelling from the hole, "Just do it. Just call the ambulance." How did that work for them? Just do it. I don't do anything unless the Lord tells me to, and I can still make mistakes.

The limits are taken off through the blood. Your faith is based on your knowledge and understanding that God is God, and you are not. *"Therefore humble yourselves under the mighty hand of God, that He may exalt you in due time, casting all your care upon Him, for He cares for you"* (1 Pet. 5:6-7). I am telling you the prosperity to get you out of debt is evading you because the demonic spirits are holding it back.

GET OUT FROM UNDER THE WORLD'S SYSTEM AND ITS LIMITS

I know people who give all the time; they tithe, and they are poor. They do not even have the tenfold return, never mind the hundredfold return. They are not even getting 1 percent back. What is it? It is the demonic. I saw that if the demonic were taken out of a Christian's life, we would wrap this up in a very short amount of time. You must turn on the devil and address him. The religious people will have a fit because they think that you can't do that. Thanks for letting me know because I have already done it. We declared war on the devil.

The limits that are placed on you are by the demonic system of the world. There is a debt system created so that satan can control people, and it took a long time for satan to get people dumbed down. I saw that satan wants people hooked on drugs, hooked on money, alcohol, pornography, movies, anything. Anything that satan can get you hooked on to get you not to respond correctly when the Spirit of God speaks to you or when you hear the word of God. The last thing satan wants is for you to discern that God is visiting you.

A partner recently told me that she believes everything I have said about the demonic. She said, "My roommate walked in as I was watching you speak live in Fort Mills. Someone else's voice came through my roommate and said, 'I don't want him on in here! Get him out of here! I don't want to hear this!' She started swearing at me and pointing at you, Kevin, on the screen and swearing." She said her roommate was the nicest girl and had never acted like this before.

The blood will separate what is operating through people and situations. You will then be able to discern the entities operating against you, and when you invoke the covenant, you will see your finances start to get set free.

> *Each of you should give what you have decided in your heart to give, not reluctantly or under compulsion, for God loves a cheerful giver.*
> —2 CORINTHIANS 9:7 NIV

Paul said to determine beforehand what you are going to give and do not give out of compulsion. God loves a cheerful giver. It is for your benefit, and you are laying up treasure in Heaven toward your account. Let us not focus on giving to get what we already have—let us give. Some people tell me that they do not have money, but do you have time? There are people I pray for every day. Pray for people. You are important to this generation.

Chapter 10

No One in Heaven Is Limiting You

Therefore, if anyone is in Christ, he is a new creation; old things have passed away; behold, all things have become new.

—2 Corinthians 5:17

N o one in Heaven is limiting you. My wife and I both fast meals to do every project we do, and everything that we do is bathed in prayer, and if I can do this, you can do this. You just have to learn how to speak from the other realm. You have to realize that all of the monetary provision that God has known that you will ever need has already been set aside for you. It has nothing to do with how good you were today. It has everything to do with how good God is and His plans and purposes for your life.

Now, there is sowing and reaping, and you know that is in the Bible, but I am not talking about that here. What I am talking about is being a distribution center. Are you the person God can come to you and say, "Can you buy this girl a bike?" Kathi and I were sitting in our living room, and the Lord spoke to us and said, "You are sowing your whole Christmas to this family." We did not know that they had six kids. I said, "Kathi, this is up to you." Of course, she was all in, and I said, "Take whatever you were going to spend on me. I want to give it to this family for their kids." We have done that every year. I am not telling you this to brag. I am trying to show you that this is why people come to read my books or hear me speak. But what about when I get to read your books and hear you speak?

It has to do with engaging God on His level, not on your level. You might think that you cannot do it. Who told you that you couldn't? Jesus once asked me that. He said, "Who told you that you could not do this?" I thought about it, and Jesus said, "No one up here is limiting you, Kevin." He said, "Everyone up here loves you, and everyone is cheering you forward. No one up here has ever spoken a word against you. No one has ever tried to hinder you. Everyone believes in you up here." He said, "It is the limitations of the earthly realm and the demonic influence on this realm that has caused you to have limitations—through the fall, through the demonic."

You could live an extra 10 to 15 years beyond what you were going to just by correcting some things in your life. You have the power to do that. You can live longer by making decisions now that sow into your future. One way to increase your life expectancy is by drinking more pure water. Jesus told me that if a 35-year-old started to drink more pure water, they could live 15 years longer.

One of the reasons people die of diseases is that the organs that are part of their immune system that filter their body wear out. The liver, the blood, and the kidneys get worn out faster because the environment is so contaminated, and these filters have to work extra hard. When you drink more pure water, it flushes your body, and it will begin to heal itself.

When Kathi and I would meditate on healing Scriptures, we would get words from the Lord on what to take to make corrections. We would go on Amazon and look it up because we did not even know what the item was. We would buy it, and we would receive healing. That is the kind of relationship that Jesus has for us. The limitations that we experience here on earth are not on us because of Heaven. They are on us because this fallen world has limitations. I once asked Jesus this question. I said, "What is it about these countries that are so poor?" Jesus said, "They rejected Me, and they serve false gods." I saw that He was right, but when you get those people to turn to God, things start to change and it starts to affect their culture.

Jesus is telling you whether you accept it or not. He is saying, "I am taking the limitations off of you." It does not mean that you will not die because it is appointed for everyone to die. That has not been broken. We are going to live forever, just not in the flesh like we are now.

> *But if the Spirit of Him who raised Jesus from the dead dwells in you, He who raised Christ from the dead will also give life to your mortal bodies through His Spirit who dwells in you.*
> —ROMANS 8:11

Paul said the same Spirit that raised Jesus from the dead is dwelling in you, and it will quicken your mortal body. Whatever happened to being a part of this principle? I let that resurrection power come from my spirit and start working its way out into my body.

I have heard my spiritual father say this while checking into a hotel. When somebody tells him no, he says, "Well, can you find me somebody who has the authority to say yes? Months ago, I paid for this room, and I have already paid for it for today. You say it's not clean, and I can't check in until 5:00, but I've already paid for today. How can you say I can't go to my room?" I had never thought about it like that, but they would not let him in. When you go to a hotel, you have already paid for it today. They said, "No, we can't do it." He said, "Well, get me somebody who can say yes. I'm waiting." Whoa! They finally found the person who could say, "Yes."

I could tell you story after story like this. I have learned so much. These are the kind of people I have above me. They understand authority because they understand that they are part of the covenant. I have had people tell me something and then say, "Why are you still standing here? You're burning daylight." It sounds like a centurion, doesn't it? The people I saw who do anything for God have centurion faith. They hear the command from Heaven, and then they give it out, and then they get people who will follow along and get it done.

WHAT HAVE YOU BEEN CALLED TO?

God has called people who are supposed to produce albums. Some are called to write songs. Some are supposed to write books. Some are called to start a ministry—ask the Lord who you are to reach. Some people have children who have been set apart and earmarked to change their generation. Some may want to become a ballerina—you pray about it, and then you help them out. Some are supposed to be artists. It's not just the painting; it is about touching lives because they are sent to that field. See how God thinks. The limitations are being taken off.

When I was in Heaven, I saw that God is more generational thinking. He is thinking about the bigger picture and about people who will come after you. Pray about what you are to do to lay in place the platform for the next generation. You can help them to do what they are supposed to do. The only reason I am doing this is that I am laying up a foundation for others. It is going to be set up so that we can wrap it up in the next generation.

I am not spending all my money on beans and rice and water. I am spending it on witnessing and helping people. I am helping children who are the prophetic generation in the womb. Satan is trying to take them out right now through abortion, but he is losing. This next generation will be that voice. Jesus will come back when the harvest comes in, and there will be multitudes coming in. I saw it starting to happen next year, and it is already happening.

The move of God is going to start, and it is going to go for seven years. When my network gets started in January, I want to get the children on there because they are the prophetic generation. I want to start to make children's programming so that when this generation comes to maturity, they will already be able to have a prophetic voice on a network. They will be able to minister to people and give the Word of the Lord and lay hands on people. I have seen this already.

I have already seen a girl in India where it has already started. People were lined up all the way out of the church building. This young girl would point to someone from 50 feet away, and they would get hit by the power of the Holy Spirit and fall to the ground shaking. She was saying, "Receive, in the name of Jesus," as she went down the line. When she was done, she was ready to go out to get some ice cream like it was no big deal to her.

I have found that children do not have the limitations that adults have because they have not been taught. However, they still have to have their parents with them to guide them and to form them. For instance, you do not tell them they cannot give. If they feel like they want to give their toy away, you teach them that it is good because they are helping someone else.

Recently we went to a pastor's church where I went to speak. The whole front row was full of ministers who came to hear me. As I looked at them, I thought I would have come to hear them speak. The entire children's program had also come in to be in that anointing, and it was so strong. The mothers had put the children across the whole back of the church, and there were about 30 kids there, and they were all coloring.

Kathi and I like to give the children money, so they all came up to receive their money and then went back to coloring. When it came time to take the offering, they took an offering for the church and took an offering for Kathi and me. The kids, one by one, started to bring their money back up. When the ministers saw that, they started giving into the bucket because the kids did.

The kids didn't hold on to their money because they discerned that what they had was given to them, so they would not lose anything. They had faith that if they gave it back to God, God would take care of them. It did not matter whether it came back to me or not because I was not thinking about that. I did not know which bucket it went in because I wasn't watching. What I was seeing was that the Kingdom of God is like that. We have to become like little children to enter in, which means taking off the limitations.

LORD OF THE BREAKTHROUGH

I do not get nervous when I have to wait, but I know that many people do. I have learned to wait on God because I do not want to make mistakes. I can wait on God. I don't have to perform. I do not have to do anything. However, I am telling you that what you are about to see on this earth through your lives will be remembered forever. The Lord God is going to bust through on your enemies. He is going to break through. Baal Perazim, He is going to break forth. In Second Samuel 5:20, David said, *"The Lord has broken through my enemies before me, like a breakthrough of water."* I can hear it right now in the Spirit.

> *So David went to Baal Perazim, and David defeated them there; and he said, "The Lord has broken through my enemies before me, like a breakthrough of water." Therefore he called the name of that place Baal Perazim.*
> —2 SAMUEL 5:20

The Spirit of the Lord is saying, "Come forth, mighty prophets, come forth out of the womb, you mighty voices. Those of you who are written. Those of you who are destined to be born. Come forth, I prophesy of the wombs of every woman all over the world. I prophesy to your wombs. I call forth the prophets and the prophetesses of God to come forth right now. I confirm what God is saying about this generation, that the children will come forth."

It is time now for the devil to finance every one of those prophets, those children, the deliverers in the womb again. Think about how many babies have died because of a demonic spirit, but he did not get the prophets. Watch what happens, and you can mark it down—watch the legislation that comes out because no one will understand it. Children are going to be so favored in their education and everything, and it is payback. Those kids will be taken care of by the Lord, and the Lord will take you out of debt to help them.

The Lord took my wife and me out of debt, but this is what we had to do. As a flight attendant, I was making almost 100,000 dollars a year. I made 2.4 million in 29 years, and we were in debt. My wife had a hair salon and worked all the time. We were working all the time, and we were still having trouble paying our bills, so something was wrong. We tithed, and we gave, and we were doing everything right. What was going on?

We knew that something was wrong because it was not adding up. We looked at everything, and we realized that the devil was ripping us off in what was going out of our household.

I said to Kathi, "I am a seed of Abraham, right? Something isn't right; plus, I have been to Heaven and back, shouldn't that count for something?" We were going through this war of debt, and it was atrocious, and this is what happened.

There were a couple of things that happened to me through the grace of God. I had bought something with short-term financing, and if I paid it off within six months, I did not have to pay any interest. I had to pay by a certain date, or they would charge me 500 dollars right off the bat. I agreed to do that, but then I went out on a trip, and while I was on the flight, I remembered that I was supposed to pay that loan.

When I got home, I called the bank, and I did not call with an attitude, and I did not try to blame it on them. Besides, they know exactly where you're at, but God does too! I was very polite, and I said, "Listen, I messed up. I was supposed to call you and transfer from my savings this amount to pay off the loan to avoid paying the interest, and I am sorry, but I messed up. Is there any way out of this because I cannot afford to lose that 500 dollars." She said, "Oh, Mr. Zadai, it says right here that at 10:10 this morning you called, and you did it already; it is already paid. It shows that you paid from your home phone." I was already out on my trip. I said, "Hey, can you send me a receipt? Thank you. Bye."

That incident was what started to show me about limitations. I said, "Lord, You just changed my past. How did You change my past? How did You just do that?" He said, "I have no limits." I asked, "Can You explain this to me?" Jesus said, "I knew that once you realized what you had done, you would repent and pray. I answered your prayer on credit and took care of it because I knew you would pray, and so I did it before you asked." He said, "I did not even get off My throne to do it." I said, "You can jimmy with the past?" Jesus said, "I have prevented your past *so* many times." When people get to Heaven, they will see where God prevented so many things from happening. So many of us focus on what did happen.

I had to ask Jesus, "How do I get out of debt?" He said, "You change your mind." I knew that I had never heard that on TV, and that is because it is in the Bible. *"And do not be conformed to this world, but be transformed by the renewing of your mind, that you may prove what is that good and acceptable and perfect will of God"* (Rom. 12:2). Be transformed by the renewing of your mind. We are so conditioned to being in debt that it becomes normal, but it is not normal. It is not normal to be in debt.

I know that people do not want to hear it. I was the same way when someone told me I should not be in debt. My reaction was, "Jack, it is none your business." Then I got to thinking about it. What is this debt system anyway? I was told by people who are above me that it was okay to have a mortgage. Then Jesus said to me, "Well, look up the word *mortgage*." So I did, and it is made up of two words, *mort* and *gage*, and it means *death grip*. That is not good, so we just declared war on the devil. We are saying, "This is the world's system, and you are the spirit of the air. This devil is how *you* operate, and it is not the way our heavenly Father operates."

God said, *"Owe no one anything except to love one another, for he who loves another has fulfilled the law"* (Rom. 13:8). He also said, *"You shall lend to many nations, but you shall not borrow. And the Lord will make you the head and not the tail; you shall be above only, and not be beneath"* (Deut. 28:12-13).

No one helped us get out of debt, and again I asked the Lord, "Lord, how do I get out?" He said, "Be an answer to someone else." I found out what my pastor's mortgage payment was for the month, and I paid for it. Then I saw that my assistant pastor's tires were bald. I worked an extra week, and I bought him a set of tires. I started being an answer to someone else.

That was in the last part of 2008. Then the markets crashed with the housing debacle, but the Lord had already told me to get out of the market, and He protected me. In January 2009, I was wondering how I was going to pay my mortgage. In February the next month, I got a notice that someone was paying our house off. The deposit went through on the fifteenth of that month. I had to wait two hours because everyone was defaulting and calling and being put on hold with Citibank because they could not pay.

After waiting for two hours and ten minutes, I finally got someone from the bank on the phone. I said, "I would like to pay my mortgage off." The representative said, "This is not funny, Mr. Zadai." I said, "I think it's hilarious." He said, "Are you serious?"

I told him, "I just need the routing number, the ABN number, and I need to pay it off before the fifteenth." "You're serious?" he asked again. I said, "Yeah." He said, "This is how much you owe, and if you get it in by the fifteenth, this is it." I made sure that it included the interest for that month, and he assured me it did and said it was completely sealed. I said, "Okay, I will give this information to the institution who is handling it, and they will wire you the money."

The money was wired, and the mortgage was all paid off. That was when I got a notice from the bank because satan does not want us out of debt, and this is how demonic it was. The notice said that I was being reported to all three credit agencies because I have defaulted on my house loan. I saved the letter because it said if I did not pay 00.00 dollars and 00.00 cents by the fifteenth, I would go into default. It would also be reported to Experian and all the others.

I had to wait another two hours to talk to someone at the bank again to tell them what happened. The rep said, "Oh, no problem, I will clear it for you." Then he said, "It won't clear." "What do you mean it won't clear it?" He said, "The computer won't let you go." That is what he said; the system would not let me go. Is that speaking to you right now? A supervisor finally got on and said, "Mr. Zadai, the only thing you can do is write a check and mail it to us for 00.00 dollars and 00.00 cents, backdated to the fifteenth of February. We will run it through and let it register it." That was what finally cleared it. The system would not let us go! The limitations have been placed on you by this system down here.

We all understand that we are going to die someday, and everyone here does that. Many people might think, "God is going to take me when He wants me to go," but that is not always the case. A pastor in Texas worked in the oil fields, and all his congregants were oilfield workers also. Many of his people got hurt in the oil fields and died, and so they were burying people all the time. When the authorities looked into it, they found that people were dying because they did not follow the work environment's safety regulations.

One of the regulations told people not to touch a high voltage electric panel unless they were standing on a rubber mat. Someone had removed the mat to wash it and had neglected to warn people about the danger. The next person to touch the control panel was not grounded by the rubber mat and was electrocuted and died. The authorities found that when the workers ignored the safety regulations, people died.

The study found out that many of the churchgoing oil workers who died had been warned by the Holy Spirit not to go to work that day but did not listen. The pastor then started to remind his people all the time to please obey the safety rules. The pastor said that from that day on, it was amazing how few people God took home. See how silly we are.

DISCERNING YOUR DAY OF VISITATION

The limitations are based on a fallen world, where there are certain laws that you cannot ignore. You can do anything once; you can jump out of an airplane without a parachute—once. You can only do all these kinds of things once. There are certain laws down here that, unless they are superseded by something else, you will be a victim of that law if you do not honor it. However, within that, God can tell you what to do to extend your life out. God can tell you what to do to prosper and stay healthy. He can tell you what you can do to save your marriage or tell you what to do to change a child's life to where they change a generation.

I have met kids who are going to be senators and doctors. I know people who will grow up and be part of something that we will look on and ask, "Who gave birth to that mighty man of God? Who was the doctor? Who is his dentist?" You see, somebody else had to help that man of God. We are all tied to the plan.

I was writing a book that has not been turned in yet because I got interrupted. The interruption was like this. I was sitting in my chair reading my Bible, and I felt a wind come by me, but there were no windows open. I have had things like this happen before, and it comes across as something physical, but it is so powerful because it is really something spiritual.

In this experience, while I was writing this book I was taken to a mountain. The page that I was typing disappeared on my laptop, and I was on a gray slate mountain with burnt rock with white on top. I saw all these amazing beings that were like elders. They were bigger than angels, but they were different. They were like Melchizedek-type people. I have seen these beings before, and when they talk to me, I say, "Yes, sir," and I do not ask questions. This time they came up to me and said, "You need to rewrite everything that you just wrote." I said, "But I just finished it." One of them said, "You did not go far enough." I thought, *I didn't go far enough?*

The elder said, "Remember what happened in Exodus twenty-three." I said, "The Lord was done with the people, and He could not be among them because they were stiff-necked, so He sent the angel of the Lord." He asked me, "What did God say to Moses about that being? Do not provoke him, because he will not tolerate your sin either" (see Exod. 23:20-21). I knew it was about unbelief because, in Hebrews, it refers to that sin as being unbelief (see Heb. 3:12-15 NIV). This Scripture is a warning for us today in the New Covenant, "Today, if you hear His voice, do not harden your hearts as in the rebellion." Christians should never be caught in that.

Can you imagine God talking about Christians like that? He referred to an Old Testament story where they fell in the desert because of their unbelief. They did not enter into the Promised Land because of their unbelief. In the Book of Hebrews, the writer tells *us* not to be like them, and he is talking to the church. The being continued to speak to me and said, "It is happening again. Go back and tell the people not to grieve their angels. The people are provoking us because of their doubt and unbelief." I had to come back and rewrite that chapter, and it turned into the book *The Agenda of Angels*.

Jesus told me to tell you this: "Do not back off. Do not be in unbelief from what you hear here because you are going to find out that you have been visited." In Jesus' day, many did not discern their day of visitation, and I saw the hurt that would come upon my life if people did not discern that there is no other move and that this is it. The moves of God were never supposed to end. I saw that we are supposed to be walking in this.

You would think as many Christians as there are in the world that we should fill a stadium with people to hear the Gospel message. Yet people will step back and say this is too good to be true, even when that is what Gospel means. The word *Gospel* means too good to be true, and it is the good news. I am saying this because I see the angels preparing your provision for everything you need, preemptively before you ask. God has already taken care of everything. I know this, and I am telling you by the Spirit of God, for you have no idea what is about to happen to you because you love God.

> *For the Lord God is a sun and shield; the Lord will give grace and glory; no good thing will He withhold from those who walk uprightly.*
> —PSALM 84:11

According to Scripture, God will withhold no good thing from those who love Him and walk in fear of Him. Do you honor God? Of course, you love Him. *"Behold, the Lord's hand is not shortened, that it cannot save; nor His ear heavy, that it cannot hear"* (Isa. 59:1). He can make something out of nothing.

A great man of God and one of the most respected people I know told me something the Lord had shown him. He said, "Kevin, your school is so much of God. When I started my school, I had 30 people sign up, so I had to shut it down." He said, "You have 6,000 students, and that is God. When you are teaching those classes, remember people will be watching those classes forever." This man of God has been to Heaven. He said, "In Heaven, you will walk by rooms, and people who did not even know you are going to be watching classes, some of them by you. Even in Heaven, we are always going to be learning. Everything you do has eternal value."

If what has happened to me happened to you, where you go to your future and see it, and you don't want to come back, but you do, then you know what is waiting for you there. You can see it in the Bible, just like we all have. But it is real to me. It is not just a hopeful thought. It is legitimately better than you can ever ask or imagine.

I saw people so happy. I can smell Heaven right now. I can see Heaven. I can taste it because the colors have a taste. The music has flavor and color, and it comes through the air on big streamers. You can see the notes just dancing as the new songs of the Lord are being played throughout Heaven. It just comes flying through the air, and people are dancing and skipping, and they are so happy.

You have jobs up there and assignments, and you are part of God's government. The frame of mind that I came back with was that I was actually in training now for the next phase of my existence, which is as an ambassador. We are all supposed to represent God, and we are all going to have our part in the new kingdom. However, I saw that I did not have to wait until I died to experience it.

I wish you could grasp this, that dying is a promotion. Dying is not something you wait for; it is something you do. Dying and living is your entrance into the supernatural. When you crucify the flesh, you die. You go under the Jordan, and you come up anew, and the life you live now is not your own, and this is for your benefit.

The demons cannot stop you. How many times do I have to tell you that the hindrances you encounter are from the demonic? As a Christian, God is not working against you. God did not make people sick and then send Jesus to heal them. Jesus went around healing everyone who was oppressed by the devil (see Acts 10:38). He healed everyone who came to Him. Everyone! He identified the need for healing as a result of satan. I saw all of this. I saw that we are supposed to enforce the blessing.

I saw that the Holy Spirit is a person who is in great authority. He is not a dove that is asking for birdseed. The Holy Spirit does not back off afraid that you might yell at Him. He is a very beautiful person, and He looks like Jesus. The Holy Spirit is very authoritative, very powerful. He is an attorney, and He gets His way. You have to yield to Him. Your will has to merge with the Holy Spirit's will because you are in a different class of being than the angels. You have to grasp this. You have to go on with God in the power of the Spirit. The Holy Spirit is an enforcer of the blessing. He enforces the covenant. He is always speaking where you are going and always speaking the blessing. He is not trashing you and not setting you up for failure.

Jesus told me, "Kevin, there has never been an angel that has been sent to you that thought they were going to fail. There has never been a time when the Holy Spirit has doubted Me. The Holy Spirit has never thought about defeat, ever." The Trinity has voted for us. That is why they bought us. We were worth it.

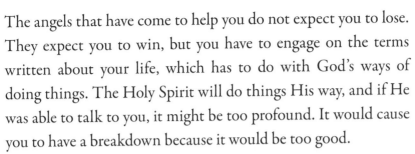

The angels that have come to help you do not expect you to lose. They expect you to win, but you have to engage on the terms written about your life, which has to do with God's ways of doing things. The Holy Spirit will do things His way, and if He was able to talk to you, it might be too profound. It would cause you to have a breakdown because it would be too good.

I know this because I prayed in the Spirit, and someone who spoke that language told me what I was saying. It was so specific that it named names and cities that I found myself in within 24 hours. At the drop of a hat, the Lord told me, "You need to go." Everything that I was saying in tongues came to pass within one day, but it was impossible. Everything fell into place without my participation mentally. It was being spoken forth through me in a supernatural way, and it bypassed my understanding, but it still came to pass.

The Holy Spirit was leading me. I realized that my interpreter told me what God had said was going to happen at 5 o'clock, and at precisely 5 o'clock it happened, in a different city that I didn't even plan on being in. Everything fell into place, and I had not even planned on being there. When I got there, I had people I did not even know handing me money. I thought, *What else am I praying in the Spirit that I am unaware I am speaking?*

> *And He said to me, "My grace is sufficient for you, for My strength is made perfect in weakness." Therefore most gladly I will rather boast in my infirmities, that the power of Christ may rest upon me. Therefore I take pleasure in infirmities, in reproaches, in needs, in persecutions, in distresses,*

for Christ's sake. For when I am weak, then I am
strong.

—2 CORINTHIANS 12:9-10

Think about the Holy Spirit being an enforcer of the blessing and speaking where you are going. Do not think you will be defeated in any way or fail because God does not think about that. We are the ones who are weak, but in our weakness we are made strong, and by the power of the resurrection, Christ has to come in.

What then shall we say to these things? If God is for us, who can be against us? He who did not spare His own Son, but delivered Him up for us all, how shall He not with Him also freely give us all things? Who shall bring a charge against God's elect? It is God who justifies. Who is he who condemns? It is Christ who died, and furthermore is also risen, who is even at the right hand of God, who also makes intercession for us. Who shall separate us from the love of Christ? Shall tribulation, or distress, or persecution, or famine, or nakedness, or peril, or sword? As it is written: "For Your sake we are killed all day long; we are accounted as sheep for the slaughter." Yet in all these things we are more than conquerors through Him who loved us. For I am persuaded that neither death nor life, nor angels nor principalities nor powers, nor things present nor things to come, nor height nor depth, nor any other created thing, shall be able to sepa-rate us from the love of God which is in Christ Jesus our Lord.

—ROMANS 8:31-39

Salvation Prayer

Lord God,
I confess that I am a sinner.
I confess that I need Your Son, Jesus.
Please forgive me in His name.
Lord Jesus, I believe You died for me and that You are
alive and listening to me now.
I now turn from my sins and welcome You into my
heart. Come and take control of my life.
Make me the kind of person You want me to be. Now,
fill me with Your Holy Spirit who will show me how
to live for You. I acknowledge You before men as my
Savior and my Lord.
In Jesus' name. Amen.

If you prayed this prayer, please contact us at
info@kevinzadai.com for more information and material.

Go to KevinZadai.com for other exciting ministry materials.

Join our network at Warriornotes.tv.
Join our ministry and training school at
Warrior Notes School of Ministry.
Warriornotesschool.com
Visit KevinZadai.com for more info.

ABOUT KEVIN ZADAI

Kevin Zadai, Th.D. was called to ministry at the age of ten. He attended Central Bible College in Springfield, Missouri, where he received a bachelor of arts in theology. Later, he received training in missions at Rhema Bible College and a doctorate of theology from Primus University. He is currently ordained through Rev. Dr. Jesse and Rev. Dr. Cathy Duplantis.

At age thirty-one, during a routine day surgery, he found himself on the "other side of the veil" with Jesus. For forty-five minutes, the Master revealed spiritual truths before returning him to his body and assigning him to a supernatural ministry.

Kevin holds a commercial pilot license and is retired from Southwest Airlines after twenty-nine years as a flight attendant. Kevin is the founder and president of Warrior Notes School of Ministry. He and his lovely wife, Kathi, reside in New Orleans, Louisiana.